A HAWKSMERE SPECIAL BRIEFING

Analyse your business

A performance health check

Carol A O'Connor, Ph.D.

HAWKSMERE
A CRONER.CCH COMPANY

Other Hawksmere Reports and Special Briefings:

Mergers & Acquisitions - confronting the organisation and people issues
Mark Thomas

Making Sense of the Social Chapter
Alan Wild

Dynamic Budgetary Control
David Allen

Evaluating and Monitoring Strategies
David Allen

Managing the In-house Legal Function
Barry O'Meara

Techniques for successful management buy-outs
Ian Smith

Employment Law Aspects of Mergers and Acquisitions
Michael Ryley

Achieving Business Excellence, Quality and Performance Improvement
Colin Chapman

Published by Hawksmere plc

12-18 Grosvenor Gardens

London SW1W 0DH.

www.hawksmere.co.uk

A CIP catalogue record for this Briefing is available from the British Library.

ISBN 1 85418 170 X

Printed in Great Britain by printflow.com

The author

Dr Carol O'Connor is founder and director of Vision in Practice Limited, a London based consultancy specialising in leadership development, business strategy and team building. She has led seminars and worked as a consultant for almost 20 years in the manufacturing and service industries and for government and the professions. Her professional services are sought by a wide range of clients located throughout Europe, the UK, the US and Asia.

Author of four highly successful management books and a frequent contributor to professional journals, she has written articles on communication, business strategy, motivation, creating vision for the future and leadership. Her writing is based on her direct experience as a consultant and trainer. Currently, she is developing a distance learning package for a leading South African publishing firm to provide leadership and management skills training to its subscribers in Africa and Asia.

Her doctorate is from the University of California where she researched communication breakdown in management teams; decision making behaviour of senior managers; and team building strategies of business leaders. She is also a faculty member for Boston University where she teaches negotiation and organisational psychology to MBA students.

Her other books are:

The Handbook for Organisational Change, McGraw-Hill, 1993

The Professional's Guide to Successful Management, McGraw-Hill, 1994

Successful Leadership, Hodder Headline, 1994

Successful Selling on the Internet, Hodder Headline, 1996

Contents

Introduction

Business performance can always be improved.This Briefing takes a proactive approach and asks company directors and senior managers to analyse their company, the way it is managed and the procedures it has in place to ensure its stability, growth and ongoing management health. This means looking for trouble so that minor weaknesses are discovered before they become major problems, and further, that larger issues are addressed in a constructive and thorough way. To guide this analysis a ***Management Health Check*** features a checklist of 80 items associated with management ill health. These items are drawn from actual businesses which have suffered serious organisational or financial difficulties.

The ***Health Check*** is divided into eight sections each one referring to an area of management which is essential to business success. This allows directors to focus on specific areas separately and also gives them a starting point for improving procedures and assessing skills. The eight management essentials are also discussed in greater detail in subsequent chapters.

Chapter 3, *Transforming the Business*, offers criteria for deciding if a symptom or set of symptoms is a sign of serious trouble or just a localised difficulty in need of a little time and attention. The emphasis here is on process improvement, a model which encourages company-wide analysis rather than isolated quick fix solutions and has the goal of in-depth business renewal and transformation. New solutions arise from new insight. Also included in chapter 3 is helicopter viewing, the role of the internal consultant and big picture thinking.

EIGHT MANAGEMENT ESSENTIALS

chapter 1

Long-term commercial viability, sustained growth and brand recognition all result from excellent management. Getting the financial numbers right plays an important part of this, but this feature alone cannot ensure overall management health. Including finance, there are eight management areas essential to business success. The organisation which develops these fully inevitably achieves prosperity because each area serves to balance and enhance the others to the benefit of all the company's operations.

However, excellent management means different things to different people, and its pursuit is often more like art than science. Experienced leaders often depend upon intuition, creative thinking, personal charisma and emotional responses when managing people and resources, but management, like art, requires acquisition of basic skills in order to produce an excellent result. High levels of proficiency in the eight management essentials featured in this Briefing appear repeatedly in case studies of successful firms. They are building blocks and the lack of even one of them will have a negative effect on the running of the business. The eight essentials for management health are:

1. vision and planning
2. commitment to quality
3. leadership
4. decision making
5. finance
6. marketing
7. communication
8. information technology

Vision and planning

Vision inspires, empowers and generates support. It invigorates activity and reminds people that there are values and issues larger than everyday business life which lend significance to what they do. Even the most junior staff member benefits from feeling a part of something greater and it is vision that generates that feeling. Vision in turn leads to strategy and development of a plan of action. A lack of explicitly stated, long-term goals seriously impairs a company's ability to grow and develop in a controlled fashion. Strategy creates efficiency because individuals then share common ground for each major decision and therefore have a basis for implementing plans.

Commitment to quality

Achievement of quality products begins with a commitment to this essential as part of the company's vision. This can be through a published quality statement with appropriate measures for quality control. Planning for quality creates an expectation of high standards and implies that performance will be evaluated in order to ensure that the standard has been achieved. These measures serve to maintain customer satisfaction and provide a baseline for future product development as circumstances change and the company grows.

Leadership

Leaders set the tone for all of the other relationships within the firm. If the example they set is poor, then this inhibits the possibility of team work and cooperation. Their attitudes also impact morale and motivation. Vacillating, non-supportive, indecisive or autocratic leaders generate an atmosphere that deadens creativity and commitment. Although leadership refers directly to the expression of power and influence, it also relates to the need to develop younger managers so they can in turn assume greater authority. Delegation and the ability to guide colleagues towards increased responsibility are valuable skills which all the best leaders possess.

Decision making

Good decisions ensure business viability and those made in isolation without reference to the needs of the rest of the business are dangerous. In general, a decision making style or approach to decision making tends to permeate a firm. This style can be highly rational at one extreme or 'seat of the pants', 'gut reaction' at the other. If a business has been successful with its choice of style, then it may seem unwise to change this. However, there are always ways to enhance, build upon and balance decision making techniques. An infrastructure of defined roles and explicit procedures eases decision making because staff know whom to consult for guidance and what steps to take to ensure their decisions serve the company's needs. Although it is difficult initially to set policies and procedures, their formulation allows routine matters to be dealt with effectively so that more important business can be given adequate time and attention.

Finance

Money talks. Whatever visions and schemes the top team may have, if the figures are not there to back this up, then failure will follow. However, finance is also an educational issue so that those who are responsible for budgeting and financial controls need communication and people skills in order to work with managers who may be less adept in this area. The

willingness to share financial data and explain its implications draws non-financial managers more fully into the planning process. Furthermore, when they understand the significance of the figures, it is easier for them to cooperate more effectively with them. Financial controls can then run more smoothly with greater managerial support.

Marketing

Marketing tells the world about the business and presents a coherent and positive image of what the company has to offer. Marketing plans best succeed when they are based on current data revealing how the public views the business. This information enables a company to deliver what customers want:, not what the company *thinks* they want. Another key aspect of marketing is implementing a growth strategy. Forming alliances with related businesses is a growing trend and encourages clarification of the company's own positive features and its contribution to its network of allies.

Communication

Business communication refers both to personal-level skills and behaviour as well as to the system devised for enabling the smooth flow of information throughout the company. Regardless of the industry, good personal communication skills always benefit a business because they ensure that the fabric of relationships stays in tact. In terms of communication systems, the advent of the flat organisation and the current wave of interest and investment in restructuring can cause serious problems unless equal attention is given to make parallel developments in communication. When layers of management are withdrawn, new communication links and new networks are needed to support the new business structure.

Information technology

For many senior managers, this area is still so novel that they remain unconcerned by all of the new developments. Unfortunately, this attitude can isolate them because electronic systems now virtually dominate the exchange and storage of information. Access to information sources world-wide, organisation of data, security and confidentiality are issues which need comprehensive planning by managers at the top of the business. If they don't understand or recognise the issues, they will be hampered when they are required to make necessary decisions.

Summary

These eight essentials provide a frame of reference for examining management effectiveness and the overall health of the business. Before completing the ***Health Check***, it may be useful to review each of these topics in turn and consider how they are expressed and interrelated in real life business.

The eight essentials for management health are:

1. vision and planning
2. commitment to quality
3. leadership
4. decision making
5. finance
6. marketing
7. communication
8. information technology

THE MANAGEMENT HEALTH CHECK

chapter 2

The questionnaire which follows is an assessment tool designed to evaluate the overall management health of a business. It is divided into eight sections each referring to one of the management essentials described in the previous chapter. The ***Health Check's*** results are interpreted so that a *low total score* shows healthy management and a *high score* indicates a need for improvement. This assessment tool gives managers a starting point for reviewing the whole of their business by discovering where potential trouble may lie.

Although each of the following items, taken separately, is not an absolute indicator of trouble, taken together they can reveal a pattern of difficulty which benefits from closer examination. As an analogy, even if an individual faints only once or is seized by unexplained coughing fits just rarely, a doctor takes this information seriously. Clusters of seemingly unrelated symptoms can indicate deeper problems and so a trivial seeming incident should at least be inspected. This is a cautious stance and yet it often proves to be a wise one.

Therefore if one of the questionnaire items describes the firm only part of the time, for the purpose of this survey, please score it as if it were fully applicable. The purpose is to stimulate thought and debate not to achieve a perfect score by discounting or minimising issues.

The management health check questionnaire

Directions

Please read each of the following items and decide if it is either *true* or *false*. An item is *true* if it relates to any event or experience during the last year. It is *false* if it has never happened or is unlikely ever to happen. Give one point to each *true* statement and no point to each *false* statement.

Vision and planning	true	false
1. The company has policy statements and operational procedures, but these are not followed.	___	___
2. Financial targets are kept secret from those who must achieve them.	___	___
3. Divisions, departments or individual managers pursue objectives which are not in line with the company's overall aims.	___	___

true false

4. Actions are taken to address isolated issues as they arise without reference to long-term objectives or strategy. ___ ___
5. Plans are made without considering the comments and reservations of those with direct experience or knowledge. ___ ___
6. Attempts to set a common direction for the firm lead to boardroom coups, power plays and avoidance of key issues. ___ ___
7. *Strategic* or *Business Plans* are produced as a matter of routine each year but are not followed or referred to again. ___ ___
8. Plans are overly ambitious or vague so that they are virtually impossible to achieve. ___ ___
9. Company leaders assume they agree about the firm's future although they never discuss what this is. ___ ___
10. The firm's current success depends upon the momentum of past achievements. ___ ___

Total Score ___ ___

Commitment to quality standards

true false

1. Rivalry among departments and staff gets in the way of running the business. ___ ___
2. Company leaders are so busy managing routine business that they fail to consider issues of long-term growth. ___ ___
3. At least one client or customer during the last year commented on the company's inconsistent service or mixed quality of work. ___ ___
4. Ongoing commitment to a quality standard depends upon the presence of individuals, i.e. if quality conscious managers were to leave the firm, then the quality programme would lose priority. ___ ___
5. The company's rapid growth makes it difficult to monitor quality. ___ ___

	true	false
6. Short-term or *fast fix* solutions are required in order to meet corporate targets and goals.	___	___
7. Customer or client complaints are handled at random and without formal procedures or assessment.	___	___
8. Pursuit of new business leaves little or no time for every day administration.	___	___
9. The word quality is used to gain client confidence and is unrelated to any company quality programme.	___	___
10. Staff training is inconsistent so that the quality of work is not entirely reliable.	___	___
Total Score	___	___

Leadership	true	false
1. Employees in essential roles resign with little warning on a regular basis.	___	___
2. Business meetings are poorly managed: they begin or run late; lack focus and direction; or end without specific resolutions.	___	___
3. Delegation is random and based upon availability rather than possession of skills or a need for skill development.	___	___
4. Powerful individuals dominate discussions so that debate is limited or curtailed.	___	___
5. Agreements are not kept between departments or between company leaders and staff.	___	___
6. Company leaders are out of touch with the concerns and circumstances of their staff, including health and safety, remuneration and fair treatment.	___	___
7. The average age of employees throughout the firm increases by one each year.	___	___
8. A 'me first' attitude is demonstrated by those in management roles.	___	___

	true	false
9. Staff appraisal is irregular and unrelated to professional development.	___	___
10. The business lacks a clearly stated reward policy and promotion criteria are not explained.	___	___
Total Score	___	___

Decision making

	true	false
1. The company is organised so that managers are uncertain about the limits to their authority.	___	___
2. Company leaders have similar, if not the same, education, training and backgrounds.	___	___
3. Decisions are made without reference to the company's long-term strategy.	___	___
4. Decisions made separately by departments risk disrupting plans made in other parts of the business.	___	___
5. In general, staff lack knowledge of the company's vision, direction and priorities.	___	___
6. Decisions regarding vital business issues are repeatedly postponed.	___	___
7. Routine issues require so much discussion time that major decisions are delayed or become rushed.	___	___
8. Removal of management layers or reduction in staff numbers causes work overload so that essential fact finding in support of decision making is not done.	___	___
9. Key employees report to different bosses without being told clearly who is supervising their work.	___	___
10. What worked well in the past is the major guide for selection of suppliers, staff development or other issues.	___	___
Total Score	___	___

Finance	true	false
1. A single individual is responsible for both financial policy and the overall run of the business.	___	___
2. Financial targets are changed or significantly altered at least once during each fiscal year.	___	___
3. Financial decisions are made at random as isolated incidents arise.	___	___
4. Budgets are produced based on last year's figures plus 10%.	___	___
5. The majority of managers do not realise how much income is needed to run the company.	___	___
6. Managers perceive the budget and the act of budgeting as an uncreative, go-through-the-motions activity.	___	___
7. Managers in decision-making positions do not know how to interpret or use financial ratios.	___	___
8. When a company's leaders discover that they are not making enough money to meet the needs of their budget, their main solution is cutting costs.	___	___
9. The finance manager or finance department works in isolation and is generally unavailable for discussion, queries or support.	___	___
10. The company depends upon short-term loans, overdraft or factoring to maintain its cash flow.	___	___
Total Score	___	___

Marketing	true	false
1. At least 25% of employees do not know what makes the business unique, special and different.	___	___
2. Decisions about product promotion are based on out of date or suspect information.	___	___
3. Managers in general are unaware that all of the their work indirectly contributes to marketing.	___	___
4. The company lacks a strategy for identifying new markets or for getting new business.	___	___

	true	false
5. The company does not know how it is perceived by its clients or the general public.	___	___
6. The average length of employment for a marketing manager is 1.5 years or less.	___	___
7. The company's brand is diluted by promotion of unrelated products or unfocused marketing campaigns.	___	___
8. Those responsible for marketing and selling are unfamiliar with the strengths of the company's products and services.	___	___
9. The marketing department is divorced from Customer Service or lacks direct access to customer complaints and comments.	___	___
10. Company decision makers do not know what their customers value most about their products and services.	___	___
Total Score	___	___

Communication	true	false
1. Messages are routinely lost from both internal and external sources.	___	___
2. It is generally necessary for outsiders to make several phone calls to different departments in order to receive the information they need.	___	___
3. Key members of management avoid or ignore each other for extended periods.	___	___
4. The company is being sued by at least one customer or client.	___	___
5. The offices' organisation or geographical location requires staff to make extra effort in order to contact each other.	___	___
6. It is normal practice to use e-mail or memos to deliver difficult news to colleagues.	___	___

	true	false
7. Outsiders receive different information about the company and its products and services depending upon who answers the phone.	___	___
8. The company lacks a policy towards ensuring that all telephone calls and letters are answered within a specified amount of time.	___	___
9. Position in the company hierarchy dictates degree of both formal and informal communication.	___	___
10. At least one senior manager has trouble speaking clearly and effectively or has a habit of inattentive, poor listening.	___	___
Total Score	___	___

Information technology	true	false
1. The company lacks a published IT security policy.	___	___
2. At least one director does not really know what the term *network* means or how to apply it.	___	___
3. Company leaders are interested in promoting the business on the Web, but do not know how.	___	___
4. Ill-advised past purchases inhibit a willingness to upgrade equipment as necessary.	___	___
5. Individuals and departments make IT decisions in isolation without reference to an overall IT development plan.	___	___
6. Individuals link their private equipment to the company's Internet connection without a security clearance.	___	___
7. The firm lacks a system for daily file backup.	___	___
8. Computer system-wide breakdown, theft or natural disaster would immobilise the company or drastically impede its ability to function.	___	___
9. Confidential files are accessible to determined staff with basic programming skills.	___	___

	true	false
10. The directors tend to agree to their IT manager's proposals without a thorough understanding of the impact of these ideas on everyday operations.	___	___
Total Score	___	___

Score summary

Each *true* answer should receive one point. Please total the number of *true* answers from each section and then transfer each of these section totals to this column. Finally, add all of the scores to discover your company's total score.

Vision and Planning	________
Commitment to Quality	________
Leadership	________
Decision Making	________
Finance	________
Marketing	________
Communication	________
Information Technology	________
Total Score	________

Interpreting the scores

A low score indicates management health and a high score shows a need for improvement.

0 to 20

This range of scores indicates robust business health and dynamic management. However, to avoid complacency, managers should review each area to look for symptoms not included in this survey.

21 to 40

Scores within this range, indicate that management practices are likely to be sound, but there is need for training in management skills and a thorough analysis of the company's business practices.

41 to 60

Firms within this range have an overall need for improvement. It could be that the firm is experiencing a challenging or transitional phase. If this is the case, then attention to vision, leadership and decision making are likely to bring benefit most quickly.

61 to 80

This range of scores indicates a very troubled firm exhibiting at least 75% of the questionnaire's symptoms. An overhaul, if it is still possible to take action, should begin with the company's leaders. Visionary, proactive dynamic behaviour is required.

TRANSFORMING THE BUSINESS

Rule of two

Rule of two analysis

The role of the internal consultant

Root cause checklist

Helicopter viewing

The *big picture*

Work in process

Process improvement checklist

chapter 3

Good business health means more than the absence of distress and negative symptoms. A recent study of leaders' views from 121 top UK-based companies revealed their belief that successful businesses have the following five features in common (see Appendix: **Winning,** DTI). These companies:

1. are led by visionary and enthusiastic champions
2. know their customers
3. unlock the potential of their people
4. deliver products that exceed their customers' expectations
5. continuously introduce differentiated products and services.

The leaders included in this study offer an ideal for healthy commercial operations, and also a profile of the achievements in their own companies. Furthermore, because the study was conducted by the Department of Trade and Industry, it provides an impartial analysis of aspirations for business success. To achieve these results, though, executives are challenged to adopt fresh habits of mind and a new way of viewing their businesses. This aids discovery of what the company needs to do in order to express positive ideals while also getting rid of negative symptoms. This chapter features techniques which aid analysts to take a broad view of their businesses so that they examine it as a complex communion of parts within a larger context.

Rule of two

Not every change requires extensive commitment of time and resources. The challenge is to identify those problems which affect the company as a whole as opposed to those which impact just one part, and furthermore determine what events are minor irritations and which present symptoms of serious trouble. The *Rule of Two* is one way to make this distinction.

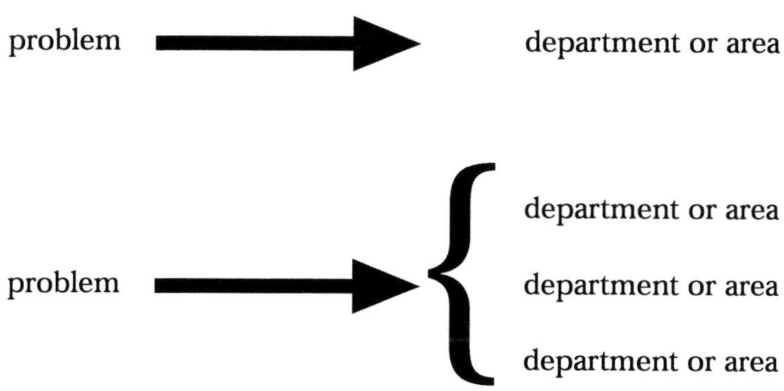

When a symptom appears in only one department or working group, then the problem is unlikely to have an impact on the whole organisation. However, departments and people are so interconnected within a business that even a minor change could also have an effect on other areas. The *Rule of Two* works best when a thorough examination is also made across departments and work groups to discover the extent of the problem.

Rule of two analysis

1. Refer to the ***Health Check***, in the previous chapter, for the management area with the highest number of *yes* responses.
2. Ask yourself if all of the symptoms from the selected area arise from a single department or result from the behaviour of a single person.
3. Ask yourself if all of these symptoms could be caused by a lack of skill or a localised organisational problem within a single management area.
4. When you read over the symptoms for the area you select, could they also be described as a symptom of trouble for a different area of management? For example, could a symptom in the *Information Technology* section just as easily be the result of a *Communication* problem as a lack of skill in IT.
5. If similar issues arise in other management areas, note where they appear and how they may be interrelated.

The role of the internal consultant

When a manager discovers symptoms of trouble, the first step is to see how they fit into the wider context of the company. The *Rule of Two* aids this process because it emphasises the need to examine whether the symptom arises from more than one department or is the result of a lack of more than one kind of management skill. Potentially serious problems need to be given extensive time and attention. Minor management problems can often be solved by training and other means. There is an old fashioned expression, 'If it ain't broke, don't fix it', which applies very well to the task of the consultant. However, the ***Health Check*** and the *Rule of Two* help determine if something is actually 'broke'.

Root cause checklist

These are the steps which contribute to the discovery of a problem's root cause and to its eventual resolution:

- Use as a starting point, the management area with the most symptoms of trouble

- Ask yourself what information you need in order to understand the problem's underlying cause
- Invite ideas from those who are either involved in producing the symptoms or who directly observe them. Disregard hierarchy and ask everyone who is concerned
- Through discussion, identify key issues and discover hidden problems
- Encourage debate to generate practical and workable solutions
- Work together to implement necessary change.

Helicopter viewing

Another challenge for managers looking for sources of difficulty in the firm is a lack of objectivity. However clear-sighted and fair minded a manager may be, it is extremely difficult for anyone to stand back from their personal reactions and offer a neutral review of the situation. It is a principle of logic that a person cannot be a part of a system and also stand outside it at the same time. Real objectivity is automatically denied any manager integrally involved with the business. There are other constraints on objectivity as well. These include:

- **pressures of time**: the urgency of priority assignments often leads to an oversight of important but less obviously pressing tasks
- **divided responsibilities**: when more than one person is responsible for a single department, tasks can be overlooked and an assumption made that someone else is taking charge
- **specialist areas**: expertise and specialised interest can limit awareness of other business issues
- **habit**: commitment to a fixed routine can result in the development of a bias against necessary change
- **background biases**: when the majority of managers share common background experiences, they can also share mistaken beliefs about management needs.

Helicopter viewing invites managers to raise their attention above their everyday activities and take a wider view of the company as a whole. Once they imagine themselves aloft, they can look down at the business below and ask:

- what issues should be addressed?
- to what standard should they be addressed?
- how to address them fully?

The *big picture*

Almost 100 years ago, the economist Vilfredo Pareto suggested that within society at large, 20% of the people produce 80% of the results.This is often referred to as the *20 to 80 ratio*. Some business leaders respond literally to this theory and seek to identify which 20% of their workforce is crucial to the business and which 80% is not.They then set about getting rid of the less productive 80%, and in the process, over-simplify to absurdity the meaning of Pareto's *20 to 80 ratio*.

Identifying high producers within a firm is always easy. It is much more difficult to determine exactly how the rest of the business has contributed to their success. For example, if the firm's high flyers lost their support network, they would become far less productive, their efficiency would decrease and ultimately so would the quality of their work.

Increased efficiency and productivity require deeper thinking than cutting away projects, activities and people which are obviously expensive or which seemingly make only a minor contribution. Every business is made up of a system of interrelated parts.Altering any single part makes an impact on the rest of the company.The *Rule of Two* is a useful test because it recognises this interconnection and helps to discover the subtle relationships and bonds between seemingly separate parts of the company.

Work in process

A management process is a set of tasks and procedures which contribute to a specific aspect of the firm's business. Some examples of business processes are mail delivery, record storage, billing and purchasing, identifiable and separate stages in manufacturing, among others.These processes work together towards completion of the firm's business and so a small change to one process can have a knock-on effect on others.The following example illustrates this.

The top management of an international accounting firm decided to set standard times for the shift schedules of all non-professional staff in their London office.This was in response to abuses they discovered with flexitime scheduling. Unexpectedly, this decision resulted in a daily pile-up of morning post in the mail room as it awaited logging and sorting by staff at their start of shift.

Because of the new scheduling rules, the mail room supervisor was powerless to mobilise additional staff or begin the work day at an earlier time although he approached the top team repeatedly with his concerns.They refused to make any exceptions and told him to get his staff to work on time. Only after irate professionals investigated the source of their late mail delivery was action taken to resolve the situation.

Process improvement needs the authority of senior managers because needed changes often require the time and attention of more than one department or set of processes. To return to Pareto's 20 to 80 ratio, a process approach examines how tasks and procedures relate to each other. When decisions need to be made to improve efficiency, recognising how the 80% contributes to the 20% helps avoid altering features of the firm which are critical to its success or, at least to its well-being.

Two points need to be considered in order to alter a process. These are:

1. identify all tasks and activities needed to complete the process
2. assess how decisions concerning one process impact the rest of the company.

Process improvement checklist

This set of questions focuses on using process improvement for decision making.

1. Think of an example of a current problem within the firm. Summarise this in two or three sentences?
2. What company wide processes are affected by this problem?
3. List all of the tasks and activities required to complete this process?
4. How does the completion of these tasks and activities affect the rest of the firm?
5. List all the other processes affected by the task and activities associated with the targeted process.
6. Reconsider the proposed decision in terms of its affect on the efficiency of all of the tasks listed.

VISION AND PLANNING

Developing vision

Mission statements

Writing a mission statement

Strategy development

Setting goals

Five business areas

Five external forces

Setting objectives

chapter 4

An inspiring vision transforms business life. People want to believe in something and vision generates the shared understanding and enthusiasm that makes going to work a positive and vital experience. Developing vision, however, takes time, concentrated effort and a willingness to question the company's traditions, values and priorities. Any reliance upon former success or a complaisance about the company's strengths gets in the way of identifying the company's future potential.

A much cited example of audacious vision is Citibank. In 1915, City Bank, the predecessor of today's world class institution, was a small bank in the Midwest United States. Its directors at that time decided that they wanted the bank: 'To be the most powerful, the most serviceable, the most far-reaching world financial institution that the world has ever seen.' Today their banking services are offered in 40 countries with over 22 million customers, a considerable achievement in so short a time.

Developing vision

Vision begins when someone says, 'Why Not?' to a highly ambitious idea; then follows this with the courage and conviction to turn that vision into reality. An essential part of this process is a willingness to explore ambitions, ideals and dreams for the future. Both hearts and minds have to be drawn into a discussion about vision so that people express what they want the company to stand for as well as what it should achieve. Development of vision takes soul searching because questions about the future can't be answered on behalf of the company without managers first addressing these issues for themselves.

The following five questions can stimulate a debate about vision.

1. What are the essential strengths of the company's products and services?
2. What qualities can be associated with these strengths?
3. What qualities should be associated with the company's work?
4. What does the business contribute to society?
5. What would be an ideal contribution in 10 years time?

These questions appeal most to those who seek meaning and purpose in what they do, but simultaneously pose a threat to those who believe dreams have no place in the office. When both extremes are represented on the board, this split in some cases cannot be bridged. However, the financial benefits of using vision to drive strategy make a strong argument in its favour so that even sceptical managers can be encouraged to see its value even if they feel unable to contribute to its development.

Mission statements

The debate about vision is the first step towards developing a mission statement. This is a short written statement describing what the company wants to achieve in the future which also indicates the company's intent and purpose. It is different from vision because it addresses a five year period and is an attempt to focus big ideas for the future into more specific areas of activity. It aims to make hopes, dreams and ambitions more concrete and applicable to everyday life. The Mission Statement is a summary of the company's long term goals and can be used to inspire commitment to a common direction throughout the business.

There can be some resistance to producing a mission statement, however, because the term has been widely misused in recent years. Many company leaders now equate it with a slick slogan, such as, 'We are first and best.' This caricature undermines the mission statement's function. However, where time has already been spent to develop a mission or resistance to its development is very great, then emphasis should be placed on implementing vision directly through long-term goals linked to its ideals. If a choice must be made, then time is better spent clarifying vision rather than debating the wording of a mission statement.

Writing a mission statement

A mission statement provides a focus for the company in five year increments. This can seem a long time period to consider in advance. However, once a discussion about future possibilities and direction is underway, then five years seems a very short span of time. Paradoxically, planning ahead increases the ability to be flexible when dealing with changing circumstances because it prepares directors to face future contingencies and explore a variety of options.

The mission statement offers *direction* to business activity, rather than *detailed goals.* It takes the form of a 30 to 50 word statement summarising long-term aims. The best missions briefly describe the who, what, when, where and how of the firm in positive and even inspiring terms. The following three statements provide examples of company missions. They are taken from real companies whose details are altered to maintain confidentiality.

> *'Our mission is to operate in the following markets: building, construction, containers and long-haul delivery.*
>
> *Our products are the best and we put our clients first. We aim to provide all our employees with job security, work satisfaction, training and above average remuneration.*
>
> *Our mission is to finance internal growth from a percentage of our profits.'*

Although all three of these statements meet the criteria of brevity, they also are potentially confusing to anyone not involved in their development and are certainly not inspiring.

For example, the first describes the firm's mission in terms of 'markets', then offers a list of business activities, not markets. The second leaves the reader guessing what kind of products the firm offers while asserting that they are the best. It also poses potential contradictions because at times putting the client first means limiting employees' job satisfaction. Finally, the third is ambiguous with the reader left to imagine the meaning of 'internal growth', the proportion of profit to be assigned to it and even what the firm produces.

The developers of these three missions put a great deal of effort into them and yet they fall far short of the ideal. All three lack imagination, a description of how the company should grow and the capacity to make a reader say, 'What a good idea.' If company directors depend upon statements such as these to inspire their staff to contribute their best effort, then they are likely to be disappointed. It would be wiser for these leaders to take time to reach agreement among themselves about the real life achievements they want the business to attain, what they truly want to do, and then write their mission statement based upon that.

Another issue is whether 'ordinary' people can write a mission statement, and, if so who should be part of the team which produces this. Slick, professional efforts engineered exclusively by external consultants cannot reflect the vision of the people responsible for the business, and it is this harnessing of vision that gives a mission statement its meaning. However, a do-it-yourself mission statement takes a great deal of effort, time and attention. Those involved can avoid some of the difficulties which attend a DIY effort if they limit the development team to those who have *ultimate responsibility* for the firm. Anyone who contributes to the content of the mission statement should be fully committed to working towards its goals until they are achieved. This means legal, ethical, moral and financial commitment.

However, employees very often offer valuable insight and therefore are a benefit to the development of a mission statement. When staff are included, they should be told in advance the limits, if any, of their influence to the process. The idea is to encourage participation, but also avoid the implication that the final wording is a matter for democratic vote. Unless this is really going to be the case, then a frank admission that their input is *a part* of the process, not a final verdict is necessary. Otherwise, hurt feelings and discouragement will be the end result, not an inspiring team effort.

Once the composition of the group is decided, the members should begin to define the firm's mission in terms of:

1. **who:**
   - a statement of the firm's legal status (limited company, plc, partnership)
   - the people who provide the product or service
   - the population targeted to receive the product or service
2. **what:**
   - the nature of the products and services
3. **when:**
   - the sense of timing the firm brings to delivery or development of its products and services
4. **where:**
   - the geographical area or country in which the firm runs or offers its business
5. **how:**
   - the quality of the firm's products and services
   - the firm's financial goals and ambitions

Every mission statement will not necessarily contain all of this information. These five questions can focus the discussion until the team reaches agreement about what points are most relevant for inclusion. The following example is taken from a baby food manufacturer's vision and addresses all of the issues in a way that has pleased directors and staff throughout the firm.

> *'Our professionally run and profitable business is committed to provide the highest quality nutritional baby foods to our world-wide base of customers while our positive work environment encourages our staff to give of their best daily.'*

The directors developed this vision after many in-depth discussions about their ambitions for the company.As a result of this, they chose to focus on infant nutrition rather than meet other consumer needs.They also decided to enlarge their markets from a regional to an international base.The words 'professionally run' and 'profitable' refer to *best management* practices which they identified as important to the firm and to the financial targets they set and which they decided to keep confidential.This example may not appeal to everyone, but it does balance both visionary and practical issues for the members of this company.

Strategy development

Strategy addresses the following three basic questions:

1. Where are we?
2. Where do we want to go?
3. How do we plan to get there?

The first two of these questions are summarised in the mission statement, or at least should be. The third is developed through the company's plan of action. When plans fill the gap between 'where are we now?' and 'where do we want to go?', then they are most likely to be implemented because the goals they include are linked to the real hopes and dreams of the strategists.

Setting goals

The next step in the planning process is to develop the goals which will bring the mission statement into reality. These goals should be fairly general and answer the question: what can we achieve in the next five years in each of the five business areas. After these goals are identified, they need to be checked for any contradictions. If after debate, opinion is still divided about setting contradictory long-term goals, then planners should return to their mission and clarify what they want.

Five business areas

Long-term goals can be set for each of the five general areas of business activity. These areas are mutually dependent and interrelated so that any development or change to one area has an impact on the others. These five areas are:

1. people
2. products and services
3. finance
4. facilities
5. marketing.

People

This area refers to both executive and non-executive staff members within the business as well as to the administrative and management systems that are used to run it.

Products and services

This area refers to what the business makes or does in order to generate income.

Finance

This area refers to the company's assets and liabilities, as well as to the system of controls in place to manage its resources and maintain its viability.

Facilities

This area refers to geographical location, physical environment (internal and external), as well as to equipment, electronic networks, and machinery. The impact of this highly sensitive area is most often ignored when developing strategy. It is vitally important because facilities' decisions play an important part in the success of every business.

Marketing and sales

This area refers to effort used to develop the company's brand recognition, increase its market share and enhance its relationship with its customers.

Five external forces

The five business areas refer to the firm's internal activities.The business is also affected by the outside environment. There are five external forces which influence the success of every organisation and all five need to be considered when developing a strategy for the business.While the company has control over internal decisions about the business areas, it has little or no control over these external forces.The challenge is to study and understand outside events so that future goals are realistic and truly beneficial to the business. Each of the long-term goals should be reviewed with reference to these five forces, which are:

1. government
2. social values
3. technology
4. consumer need
5. competitors

Government

This area refers to political activity of every sort, including taxation, legislation, health and safety requirements and even terrorist activity.

Social values

This area refers to health, education, morals, ethics, and social class issues. Awareness of social thinking is essential when making major decisions about the business. This includes anticipating the impact of peoples' changing attitudes towards what the company offers the community.

Technology

This area has an increasing influence on all aspects of business. It refers not only to equipment innovations, but also to new applications for database management of any kind, and of course intranet and Internet links.

Consumer need

This area refers to customers; who they are; what they want; and where they are located. This includes an awareness of potential needs as well as those already identified with consideration given to demographic shifts as well as to changes in social values and trends.

Competitors

This area refers to all sources of competition not just those within the company's own industry.

Setting objectives

From vision to mission to goals, planners consider the company's future in broad and general terms. To ensure that specific actions are taken to achieve these ideas, short-term objectives spell out the individual activities needed to develop each long-term goal. The two following definitions distinguish between goals and objectives.

A goal is a general and realistic aim for long-term achievement.

An objective describes a specific result to be achieved within a limited period of time. Objectives lead to the accomplishment of goals.

Objectives lead to achievement of the company's long-term goals and each one needs to be reviewed in order to discover any contradictions or repetitions of effort shown in other objectives. In this way planning activity is orchestrated so that objectives harmonise, blend and integrate to serve the overall growth of the business. Every objective should include each of the features listed here. Objectives should be:

- **consistent**: they must integrate well into other aspects of the plan
- **specific**: they must state exactly what end result is desired
- **measurable**: they must be described so that it is possible to present tangible evidence of their achievement by a named person who is accountable for results
- **related to time**: they must have a deadline for their completion
- **attainable**: they must be realistic in terms of available time, energy and resources

Once objectives are set for each goal, then specific actions can be decided towards achieving that goal. This process is aided with the following questions:

- What actions does this objective require?
- What details must be included?
- How should this be communicated? To whom?
- Who is responsible? To do what? By when?
- How is the action to be monitored?

The answers to these questions lead to a detailed list of things to do with the final stage of the process actually accomplishing them.

COMMITMENT TO QUALITY STANDARDS

Quality service

Total Quality Management: TQM

Benchmarking

Growth issues

The balancing act

Creating a balance checklist

chapter 5

A commitment to a quality standard requires long term thinking and a belief that the considerable investment needed will eventually bring a worthwhile return. These are some of the benefits a quality programme offers:

- customer satisfaction
- improved brand image
- increased and sustained sales
- recognition as an industry leader.

Quality service

Initiating a quality standard programme can be expensive. In manufacturing it can mean, among other issues, increased reject rates, and in service industries, additional time-consuming procedures. These issues and their expense deter some directors from making a commitment to a formal quality programme, particularly if they believe their goods and services are of a good standard already.

The issue is whether a quality programme actually increases profits. In fact, the test of time shows that quality initiatives which are well planned and have full commitment from company leaders bring great benefit to the business, both long and short term, through increased productivity, efficiency, reliability, profits and improved motivation throughout an entire work force. Those companies making an explicit commitment to quality service gain increased attention just from the announcement. When they deliver what they promise, they then gain new levels of appreciation and an improved image. Word of mouth promotion is always a powerful endorsement, and quality performance encourages this.

There are other benefits as well. A published quality policy not only impresses customers, it also affects staff. People like being associated with a quality oriented company and they know that the firm's good reputation reflects favourably upon themselves. A sense of *esprit de corps* based on a positive company image leads to decreased absences and complaints of stress. Another indirect benefit is enhanced stature for the firm. When problems arise, suppliers, clients and others are more likely to seek resolution in a constructive manner. Firms with quality programmes in place are likely to be assumed innocent until proven guilty.

However, short term or superficial quality projects are worse than none at all. When customers are promised quality, they are prepared to be more critical of any failings which they do discover. Furthermore, a cosmetic initiative demoralises staff. They can feel confused and disoriented because they no longer know what performance standards they are meant to follow.

Total Quality Management: TQM

TQM is a far-reaching quality programme which requires everyone within the firm to examine issues of quality performance. It leads, in most cases, to a thorough evaluation of the company's values and beliefs so that complete change is created in the way the firm conducts its business. The TQM firm is customer centred and quality focused with every employee taking responsibility for this. The model for this initiative is frequently presented as a triangle, so that the three essential features of the TQM approach are given equal weight. These features are: management commitment, motivated work force and measurement of quality (see Figure 1 below).

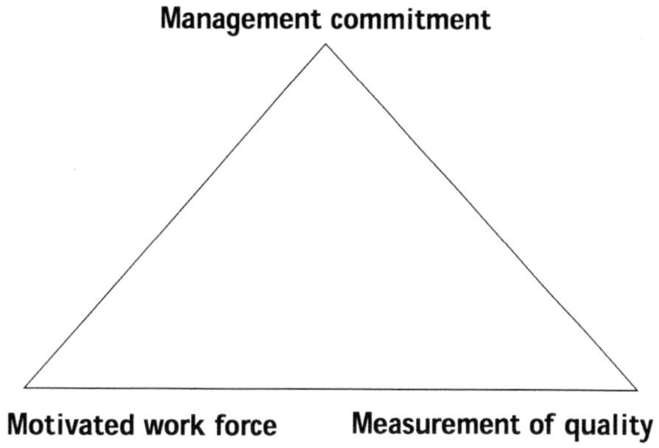

Figure 1: Total quality management model

All three issues are addressed when creating an environment for actively promoting quality. However, each firm is unique and so a TQM programme has to be developed to meet each company's individual needs. The final result is the same for every firm, that is, a shared culture based on a commitment to quality through continuous improvement. Culture in this context refers to the firm's values, knowledge base and its experience. To create a quality focused culture, the firm should:

- express a commitment to quality as part of the company's vision
- set out procedures which achieve this in the strategic plan
- develop a common language for quality
- provide ongoing education and training for skill development.

TQM needs the active participation of the company's top managers because they can offer the structure, resources and show of enthusiasm that can inspire staff to take part in full. This programme leads to profound change because after investing so much time, energy and finance, those involved tend to follow through in order to get a yield on all of their

effort. Guidelines for achieving TQM are provided in a British Standards Institution publication, *BS 7850 Part 2* (see Appendix). This standard is the British adaptation of International Standard 9004-4 published in 1993.There are four actions which contribute to a successful TQM programme. Each is of equal importance to the achievement of quality awareness.

1. A survey of all firm members should be made to discover the current attitudes and commitment to quality. This not only provides valuable information, but also establishes a baseline against which future attitude change can be measured.The survey items should establish the extent of quality awareness: where this awareness already exists and where it needs to be developed.
2. The company's most senior manager should make a clear and public statement that quality is a way of life for the business. A reference should be made to this commitment in the mission statement and also in a public endorsement of the value the company places on quality.
3. Everyone in the firm should become involved in discussions about quality and actively explore how this initiative affects their own work. Where training needs are identified, action should be taken to provide the necessary skills. Education and training are integral parts of a quality programme.
4. Performance should be monitored with a view to creating continuous improvement. TQM is successfully implemented when everyone takes responsibility for monitoring the quality of the company's work.

Benchmarking

A benchmark is a point of reference which is used to evaluate or measure the achievement of a standard. In business, the term is widely used to refer to objective criteria which define *best practice* for an area of activity. Although individual firms develop benchmarks in cooperation with other companies, increasingly they are established by non-partisan organisations, such as professional bodies, business institutes and government agencies committed to supporting trade and industry.

In general, these groups gather data from companies in cooperation with the following principles:

- **confidentiality:** sources of data are kept anonymous
- **intentionality:** agreement about who will see the data and how it will be used
- **contact:** communication between participants follows agreed guidelines
- **legality:** legal issues and limitations are defined.

A benchmark can be used in two ways:

1. within an individual industry so that companies can compare their performance against their competitors without loss of confidentiality
2. across a variety of industries so that a company compares specific areas of their industry's business practice against the way that leading firms in other industries perform in those areas.

Benchmarking is most easily applied to quantitative or measurable business features, such as costing and manufacturing specifications. However, it is also very beneficial to use benchmarks to establish performance standards for communication and management systems, customer service and decision making practices among other issues.

Establishing benchmarks for management functions and activities can be achieved by:

- identifying which management area can benefit
- identifying the core skills and essential behaviours needed to serve that area
- identifying the recognised industry leaders for each area to be benchmarked
- measuring this industry leader's performance in terms of the core skills
- measuring the company's own performance and identifying the gaps between its results and those of the industry leading firm
- establishing a programme of change to achieve new performance standards
- monitoring the change until the benchmark is achieved.

Growth issues

A company's rate of growth has a direct impact on its ability to maintain a quality standard. When presented with a growth opportunity, directors at times need the discipline and courage to say, 'no' to those schemes which look beneficial but do not serve the company's mission or its current interests. These include badly timed mergers, capital purchases when cash is tight or the acceptance of high risk business when the client list is already risk-laden. Like bargains, opportunities offer value only when they are timely, genuinely desirable and advantageous. However, without a crystal ball it is always difficult to distinguish a good opportunity from an ill-advised venture before the choice is actually made.

Businesses which lack a system for evaluating growth opportunities risk investing time, money and energy in mistaken ventures. This kind of firm grows by following a line of least resistance, by random chance or by changing circumstances. Even if routine business is managed with extreme efficiency, because growth issues are not managed, then under-

performance results. Decisions about the company's future need conscious choice rather than default.

The balancing act

Successful business leaders have the ability to shift their attention from short-term administration needs to focus on long-term strategy. When managers lack this essential skill, they can become bogged down in burdensome detail or, alternatively, caught up in pursuit of unrealistic ideas. One way to analyse managers' ability to balance administration with vision is to organise information about how they use their time by plotting this on a matrix. The matrix then highlights visually the amount of time that is used for administration as opposed to strategy development.

The matrix is completed by recording along the vertical axis the names of all the managers with significant decision making authority. Then across the horizontal axis, there are two items: first, a record of the number of hours spent doing administration, and second, the amount of hours spent on strategic or growth issues. In professional firms this information is recorded as normal practice; in industry time recording data is less readily available. However, an analysis of this information can reveal which managers avoid *delegating* routine work as well as which avoid *doing* routine work in order to focus exclusively on idea spinning. Figure 2 shows an example of this matrix and Figure 3 plots the relationships in graph form.

Managers' names	**Administration hours** (average per week)	**Strategy hours** (average per week)
A	5	5
B	2	5
C	5	1
D	3	3

Figure 2: Balancing short and long term needs

Manager **A** gives an equal amount of time to both administration and strategy. In contrast Manager **C** gives only one hour to strategy and 5 hours to administration. Because situations vary from business to business and from one management specialist area to another, it isn't really appropriate to suggest an ideal balance for these two important management functions. However, company directors can set a benchmark (see previous section) of what they believe to be a healthy balance for their company and ask their colleagues to monitor

their use of time towards achieving this. Alternatively, they can open a debate so that an awareness is raised for the need to be conscious of achieving this balance week by week and throughout each quarter.

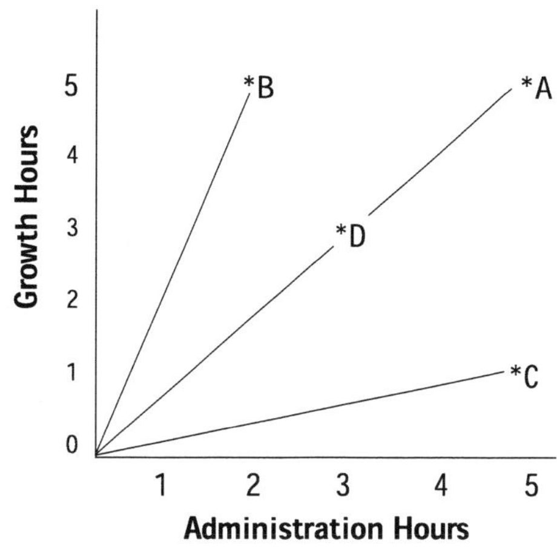

Figure 3: Graph of the balance

Creating a balance checklist

The following questions highlight issues relevant to balancing everyday business with creating long-term strategy making.

1. Are the firm's managers, in general, driven by their ideals and ambitions?
2. Are the firm's managers, in general, practical people?
3. Do managers realise they should balance administration with strategy development?
4. Is there a forum in which managers can debate or seek clarification about long-term strategy?
5. Is the firm's every day administration run effectively?

LEADERSHIP

chapter 6

More than anything else, a business needs good leadership. Management of resources and coordination of activities are also essential, but the top team needs people with that added spark so that they take charge in a consistent, comprehensive and inspiring manner. Currently there is a tendency for those in positions of power to resist proclaiming themselves 'the leader'. It is a title used at an annual dinner to praise a colleague's work, or softened with qualifications such as 'party leader', 'team leader', or 'project leader'. Even the ruthless and highly ambitious avoid stating publicly that leadership is their aim in life.

Although idealistic teachers continue to promote the qualities of leadership in schools, and academics conduct research into leadership in universities, those who carry leadership responsibility in public can be diffident about saying, 'I am the leader!' Certainly, this title is held in less repute than it was at the start of this century. This isn't surprising given the gruesome abuses of power seen in world politics. For many people these abuses are associated with the *function* of leadership rather than the *personalities* of specific leaders.

As always, talented, powerful and astute individuals continue to assume the roles of director, manager, administrator and supervisor, but tend to use greater subtlety than their predecessors when referring to the extent of their influence. However, leaders who avoid asserting their legitimate authority with clarity and confidence often provoke confusion and anxiety among their colleagues. They create a vacuum where there should be a focus for constructive and representative authority. By not acknowledging their own power, they disempower others because their colleagues lose their representative, guide and coach. These essential leadership functions are unfilled when 'nice guys' refuse to take full responsibility for their leadership role.

Truly nice guys, both men and women, are more honest about themselves and to others. Assuming a mantle of legitimate authority in a responsible manner invites colleagues to debate and challenge that authority in the interests of the business. The art is to make a firm stand in such a way that colleagues are allowed, if not invited, to respond with strength in return.

Leader and follower paradox

A modern definition of leadership emphasises the mutual dependence between leaders and followers. Essentially, this acknowledges that without followers there are no leaders. Although their responsibilities are different, the contribution of both roles is crucial to any group effort. The following definition highlights this idea. It suggests that leaders may develop a vision, but their supporters must be willing to accept it and act jointly to achieve it. Otherwise, leadership is just an illusion.

Leadership is the ability to present a vision so that others want to achieve it. This requires skills to build relationships as well as to organise resources.

However important and powerful business leaders may be, they are wise to remember that the pinnacle of any hierarchy rests upon the bottom step of some other larger hierarchical grouping. No leader is all powerful or free from the influence of others as is illustrated in Figure 4. The president of a multinational corporation answers to shareholders. The politician depends upon voters to remain in power. Even the totalitarian ruler, supreme within a single nation, eventually has to face the international community as a small fish in a large pond. Having attained the peak of influence, leaders quickly discover the constraints placed upon them. Those who forget this, risk isolating themselves and their companies from new challenges and outside influences.

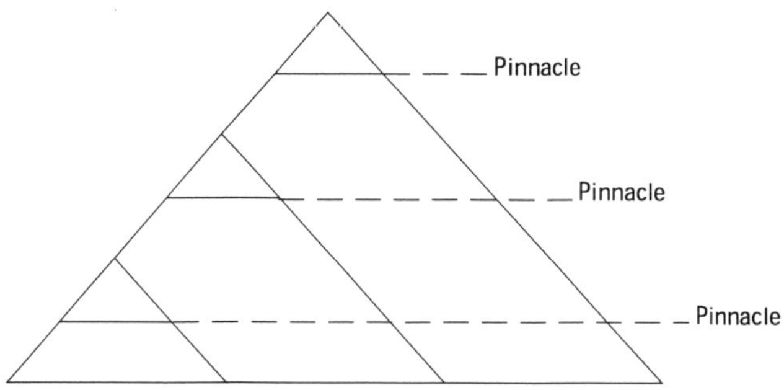

Figure 4: The 'top' is relative

Top business leaders not only have to exercise authority, they also need the wisdom and tact to accept others' leadership on occasion and follow them. The skills associated with following lack glamour and yet, paradoxically, contribute to the kind of leadership which produces results. These skills include the ability to: receive advice and guidance, obey legitimate constraints, listen carefully to colleagues' ideas, acknowledge power in others, and when appropriate, express humility.

Leaders who possess skills of 'followership' are able to cooperate with the ideas and insights of their colleagues. The direction they offer is therefore based on collective wisdom not just their own ideas. Old fashioned and autocratic leaders are threatened by the very idea of discussion or debate referring to this approach as weak and vacillating. This is because they equate being powerful with maintaining maximum control over their audience while holding centre stage at all times. This is a cult not a company. The best and ultimately the strongest leaders are always in touch with their colleagues' views and are secure enough to allow themselves to give in and recognise when someone else is smarter,

greater, braver and more right than they are on any single occasion. Furthermore, it is a tactic that builds strong alliances.

Power and politics

Power is both fluid and fixed at the same time and holds the possibility for those who possess it to increase or decrease their power without necessarily affecting their colleagues' ability to be powerful as well. Effective leaders recognise the sources of their power as well as its limitations. This enhances their ability to assess their own potential for achieving, projects schemes and ideas. For some leaders, this assessment occurs so rapidly and automatically that they refer to it simply as instinct. Others evaluate power and the powerful both consciously and rationally. Whatever method they use, managers benefit from recognising just where they are placed 'on the food chain'.

Sadly, those who lack this skill stand among the arrogant, the rude, the bumptious, the self-deluded, the impractical, the naive and the innocent in that order of self-menace. As leaders, their lack of awareness is an imposition upon other peoples' tolerance and understanding rather than a contribution to a successful business. Ignorance about power, its uses and deployment is an inappropriate quality in any professional because it undermines judgement and leads to error.

There are four kinds of power most commonly exercised within organisations. These are:

1. designated, also called legitimate power
2. expert power
3. charismatic power
4. information power

Leaders who exercise all four kinds are virtually unstoppable. Those who are committed to achieving their projects and goals gain by choosing to increase their power and influence through learning to exercise additional kinds of power. For example, there are experts in their field who believe that facts should speak for themselves so that it is inappropriate to 'use politics' to influence decisions about their projects' future. However, they increase the likelihood of a positive response to their proposals by choosing to draw upon sources of power beyond their personal expertise (expert power). This can include presenting their facts thoroughly and effectively (information power) and using a small amount of charm when they do so (charismatic power). The overall effect of three kinds of power, consciously employed, is far more influential than dependence upon just one.

Designated power

This kind of power is linked to specific roles or positions within the company. The firm's organisational chart indicates all of the positions which have designated power. Also associated with designated power is the authority to reward or punish, to coerce or encourage.

Expert power

This kind of power exists separately from designated power and is linked to the level of skill, accomplishment and achievement each individual possesses. It increases through personal effort so that learning new skills and developing further expertise adds to this kind of power. Unfortunately, expert power is not always fully recognised in business because it is most often revealed through reports, teaching, professional writing, lecture giving, and research.

Charismatic power

This source of power is linked to personality and is essentially the ability of one person to influence another through force of will, humour or charm. Charisma emanates from some people and not from others. In traditional theories of leadership, charisma is an essential trait. However, dependency upon charm, style and grace can be dangerous. Charisma backed by expertise is a more winning formula.

Information power

This kind of power is vitally important to the functioning of the business. It is found in databases, files, documents and the memories of long serving staff at all levels of the business. The sudden loss of one of these sources of power can mean communication breakdown within the company. Management of information is now as vital to business success as the management of finance.

What is empowerment?

Empowerment is both an ability and an attitude which leads to shared responsibility for achievement and authority for decision making. It works by encouraging colleagues to believe in their own effectiveness and increase their sense of having a choice about how they complete their work. Empowered staff feel enriched and are highly motivated.

It is often believed that managers and staff alike can become empowered overnight. This is far from true. Particularly, where there is a fixed and formal chain of command, managers

can fear reprimand if they risk taking the initiative *even if they are asked to do so.* Also many staff may not know how to behave in an empowered way or may not wish to accept the increased responsibility.

What are the risks?

- Untrained staff can develop a false sense of confidence and make errors of judgement.
- The shift to an empowering leadership style causes many managers to feel stress as they learn to delegate and manage staff in a new way.
- Crucial deadlines can be missed as staff learn new responsibilities.
- Skills and competencies need identification for each newly empowered role so that staff can be trained to function successfully.

What are the benefits?

- Greater efficiency as staff pull together as a team in a positive work environment.
- A highly motivated work force which *wants* the business to succeed.
- Increased commitment based on a sense of shared responsibility to get things done.
- Job enrichment from the top down as staff grow and develop to meet new challenges.

Empowerment style survey

Please answer *yes* or *no* to the following questions.	**yes**	**no**
1. When sought for advice, you ask colleagues and staff to clarify fully what *they* think is best before you respond.	☐	☐
2. You encourage discussion of policy and procedure among your staff.	☐	☐
3. When leading meetings, you do not intervene or guide the discussion.	☐	☐
4. Your staff frequently express satisfaction with their work.	☐	☐
5. You keep people guessing about what you are going to do next.	☐	☐
6. Your staff and colleagues form cliques and factions so that they ostracise those whose 'face doesn't fit'.	☐	☐
7. Your staff and colleagues make their preferences known openly and spontaneously.	☐	☐

	yes	no
8. You believe that creative and empowered professionals do not wish to have leaders.	☐	☐
9. Everyone knows that your favourite colleagues and staff receive special treatment.	☐	☐
10. You call a meeting to decide an urgent issue and no one attends.	☐	☐
11. When you are away from the office, the overall productivity decreases.	☐	☐
12. Factions among your colleagues and staff make it impossible to make even vital decisions.	☐	☐

Analysis of results

A 'yes' answer to items:

1	2	4	7	indicates an empowering approach.
3	8	10	12	indicates a vacillating approach.
5	6	9	11	indicates a disempowering approach.

This checklist can give a general sense of the approach to leadership style which you may usually choose to use. Only the *yes* answers contribute to a tally of your score because *no* answers could indicate one of the other two approaches.

For example, a *yes* answer to *item* 1 indicates an empowering approach. A *no* answer could indicate either a vacillating or disempowering style because *not asking* a colleague to clarify what they mean before giving advice could be the result of an inability to give direction as well as a lack of interest in their views.

The adaptive leader

Categorising styles of empowerment is a first step in assessing leadership behaviour. It allows individuals to consider their general behaviour and then adopt specific actions to suit varying work situations. In recent years, the management consultants Paul Hersey and Ken Blanchard proposed a model for effective leadership that is widely adopted throughout industry. Much study went into developing their system, which helps leaders to decide the kind of leadership behaviour best suited to each situation. Their model suggests

that groups go through a four stage process of maturation. These stages are: 'telling, selling, participating and delegating.'

Each of these stages requires different leadership styles. Stage one begins with the group's formation. Hersey and Blanchard suggest that effective leadership at this stage means strong and directing behaviour so that the leader tells group members what to do. The emphasis within the group is on completing tasks as well as learning work-related skills. Most interaction occurs between the leader and individual members of the group who at this early stage are not yet well acquainted with each other.

Later, as the group becomes increasingly skilled at its work, it needs leadership which encourages group members to develop good relationships among themselves. Although the completion of a task is the reason for forming the group, the leader also wants the group to work well together. During this second phase of group maturation, leaders aid group communication and promote mutual understanding.

During the third phase, group members are becoming both technically competent and personally comfortable within their group. The leader's task is then to find a balance between relationship formation and task completion. Group members at this stage can challenge the leader's ideas and also discuss completion of tasks among themselves towards improving their productivity and the quality of work. They also begin to participate in group leadership. In this model, during the fourth and final stage, group members require little direction from their leader. They are now so competent and work so efficiently together that the leader can delegate completion of the group's tasks to them.

Hersey and Blanchard call their model 'Situational Leadership'. Essentially, they suggest that leaders should evaluate the maturity of their group and its members and then adapt their leadership to serve the needs of each situation. In principle this is an excellent idea; in practice it is very difficult to achieve. The challenge is knowing how to assess the level of maturity: of the group itself and of its individual members. If this is accurately assessed, then the leader must also match the right style to serve the group's stage of development.

These are not easy tasks and they presuppose a great deal of personal insight, wisdom and skill. They also assume that leaders have more control over people, resources and time than they normally have in everyday working situations. Systems, methods and theories are only as useful as their practitioners are self-aware. However, the model provides a guide for analysing a group's circumstances and is therefore helpful towards adapting leadership behaviour to meet changing group needs.

Delegation: art and science

Delegation provides a useful tool for empowering staff, getting more work done and also training junior staff to assume more responsibility. Its skilful exercise requires method and commitment beyond passing unappealling work on to others. There are four steps to effective delegation. Each is important for developing expert staff and building a team.

Define the task

This step is an obvious one because it sets the limits and scope of each assignment in clear and specific terms. An effective way to introduce the task is to ask what the delegatee already knows about it and what suggestions would aid its completion.This process is often called 'creating ownership'. Good delegators encourage people to feel responsible for the success of their work so that they 'own' its achievement themselves.

Explain why the task is important

When under pressure, this step can seem an unnecessary use of time. Explaining the 'big picture' of an assignment is crucial, though, particularly for those who are just learning because it allows them to complete the task without constantly having to seek advice. When this step is ignored or overlooked, delegators open the way to increased chance of error. Explanation encourages understanding, interest and involvement, and people who have an idea of what the task should look like when it is completed bring a greater sense of purpose and clarity to their work.

Make clear any expectations

This step includes describing the kind and amount of responsibility those delegated are given in order to complete the task.The limits of their authority should be explained as well as the circumstances under which they should seek advice and how they will be evaluated when the task is completed. This also implies that they should be told when, where and how they can reach the delegator for further information. Delegators create serious problems, if not crises, when they delegate and then disappear.

Monitor and evaluate progress

This step refers to the delegator's ultimate responsibility for the completed task. If progress is monitored effectively there is a double yield: the work is done and also the person delegated to has a sense of achievement with lower risk to the firm. If expectations have been explained in advance, then the harsh edges of a performance review are removed and performance standards have a sense of fairness.

DECISION MAKING

chapter 7

The benefit of hindsight

With hindsight, disastrous decisions always seem to have been avoidable with their outcomes so obvious that their originators appear consciously to have chosen catastrophe. The following three examples provide illustrations of this:

Example 1

A construction project ran into unforeseen difficulties, so that its overrun costs were likely to be £5 million per week. The project leader immediately informed his employer, a firm of construction engineers, on learning the scale of their potential loss. He firmly believed that the construction project could not be completed and said so.

Although their client, a consortium of developers, was told, the consortium feared that news of the project's failure would cause the banks to call in their loans. They chose not to make a decision at that time and the project costs escalated. The firm of construction engineers carried on with the project, thereby colluding with the consortium.

Example 2

In the 1960's, an architectural firm developed plans for a 40-storey mirror sided skyscraper and promoted this as the first ever computer-designed building with human input on design being kept to a minimum. Meteorologists and construction engineers warned the developers against using a newly developed glass for that location and kind of structure. However, this advice was ignored and the building went ahead as planned.

On the first occasion of a gale-force wind, the sheets of glass panelling shook loose from their sidings, shattered and fell to the streets below. Luckily no one was hurt. After urgent meetings, an emergency solution was decided to substitute wood panels for the glass until a new window material could be made available.

Example 3

A group of medical doctors gained government funding for a famine relief project. In spite of warnings from representatives of an international health organisation, they entrusted distribution to local stewardship with criminal associations. Later, the doctors discovered that there was massive misappropriation of funds, medicine and supplies.

Lacking management skills, their attempts to correct the situation drove the few honest brokers away and encouraged the dishonest ones to use even more covert means to carry out their theft. The doctors decided to carry on even though they realised that only 20% of donations reached the people in need. They feared that adverse publicity would dry up funding entirely and they felt committed to their project.

In all three of these examples, the decision makers received clear warnings of potential disaster. With hindsight it is easy to see the right course of action for each group to have followed.

Example 1: The construction engineers should have withdrawn their expertise before more unrecoverable costs were incurred.

Example 2: The architects should have listened to advice from human experts given the rudimentary nature of early *expert system* software programs used to design the building.

Example 3: The doctors should have stopped distribution of supplies and thoroughly reorganised their systems.

Instead, they all chose to go ahead because, at the time, this seemed to be the best choice available to them. These examples are based on real life events and the actual outcomes brought financial ruin to the first example, ridicule and law suits to the second and professional disgrace to the the third. Although these examples are more dramatic than those facing managers in everyday life, the underlying issues are the same: when to say 'stop', when to take advice and when to reorganise and start again. Decision makers require more than techniques, they also need to adopt a *kind of thinking* which challenges self-delusion, and further, to create the *kind of organisation* which makes effective decision making a standard practice.

What undermines objectivity?

The work of Herbert Simon, a Nobel Prize winning economist, suggests that human beings in general are limited in their ability to be objective and make rational decisions. He called this *bounded rationality* and argued that subjective forces such as perception, bias, intelligence and experience are the natural drivers of decision making rather than rational analysis. This is important to recognise because people absorb and use information for decision making according to their abilities. Rational decision making requires the assimilation of unlimited amounts of data and this is beyond the capability of human beings. To the extent that managers recognise this *essential limitation* to their objectivity, they can then assess how it has an impact on their review of factual evidence and thereby increase their objectivity.

To paraphrase Herbert Simon, subjective influences occur in the decision-making process in at least three ways.These take place when decision makers automatically or instinctively:

- repeat what worked in the past
- choose the first solution in a series of choices which seems to work
- settle for a close approximation of what is really needed.

On occasion all or one of these influences lead to making the right choice. However, the key issue for decision makers is to be aware of what they are doing so that they act more consciously as a result. They increase their objectivity by recognising the powerful influence subjective reactions have on the way people make choices.They can then build into the decision making process ways to deal with this irrationality.

Irrationality

Certain situations are so dynamic that the information collected in aid of decision making is contradictory, ambiguous or limited.An objective analysis of poor quality data can be time consuming and result in guesswork masquerading as analysis. An alternative approach openly declares that the available information is weak or incomplete so that it is an obvious necessity to interpret the data with care before any resource commitments are made.This is common sense, but in practice, some managers get carried away during the decision making process.

For example, managers may be asked to approve a promotion campaign aimed at reaching new customers. Where demographic research is available and market surveys have been conducted then these numbers help to identify potential market share gains. However, if any of the available data is out of date, of suspect accuracy or based on estimates and projections only, then managers should discuss how to extract value from the data and then identify the level of risk they assume if they make any of their decisions based on this data. This step to control data usage serves to limit the impact of irrationality.

An antidote

The following steps contribute to effective decision making so that the individual limitations of the decision makers are addressed. It is an enhanced version of the steps generally included in rational decision making processes.

- gather all available information
- define the problem
- recognise in *advance* any resource limitations

- ask, 'What action would I never take?' as an antidote to bias
- confer with colleagues
- act on the decision
- ask: 'Was the solution aimed high enough?'

Two kinds of decisions

There are two kinds of decisions: programmed and non-programmed. Programmed decisions refer to routine matters while non-programmed decisions require more time and concentration. When managers are under pressure of time, research shows that they tend to make programmed decisions first, thus 'clearing their desks' for issues which require thought. Unfortunately, when time runs out or the manager has become exhausted, the non-programmed decisions receive last minute attention and can even be left incomplete. This is an additional issue to consider when ensuring that decisions are as rational as they can be. (Balancing the need to administer the business with the requirement to think strategically is addressed in the chapter, *Commitment to Quality*).

Challenging the status quo

Recent research from the Cranfield School of Management (see Appendix) says that one way to create business success is to develop individuals who have the potential to innovate and challenge the way things have always been done. Managers who develop expertise in each of the following areas offer real benefit to the business:

- **managerial knowledge:** learning how the business operates
- **influencing skills:** leadership, mentoring, communication
- **clear thinking:** understanding how others think and translating complex issues into action
- **self knowledge:** awareness of who you are and how others see you
- **emotional resilience:** coping with pressure, managing personal responses, allowing emotion to make a positive contribution to the business
- **personal drive:** maintaining steady and consistent levels of motivation regardless of career stage

Companies which encourage innovative managers create the kind of organisation where effective decision making is a normal practice. Healthy challenge to the status quo is an insurance policy against the kind of decision making illustrated in the examples at the start

of this chapter. Confident, clear thinking managers are also less likely to leave complex issues undecided while they debate parking space allocation or other routine matters.

Organisational structure

Another major influence on decision making is the way in which the company is organised. All of the interrelated roles from the top to the bottom of the business form a skeletal structure. When this is well designed, the company is able to function effectively with decision makers clearly identified and empowered to act. The most commonly used structure found in business is the hierarchy (see Figure 5) with decision making authority increasing towards the top of the structure.

Hierarchy

A hierarchy is beneficial for businesses where work is organised into tasks which are further divided into segments or sub tasks. Mass production emphasised the use of a tall and thin organisation because the division of labour in manufacturing requires many people to complete sub tasks rather than a single person to complete a series of tasks. When several individuals work together to complete task segments, then this increases the need for managers to coordinate their work and monitor the overall completion of the task. Each layer of management contributes to the height of the hierarchy.

The basic hierarchy model looks like this and is repeated in the majority of corporations around the world.

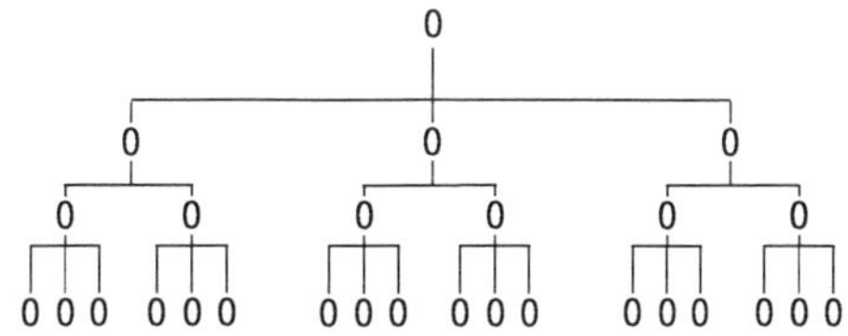

Figure 5: Traditional tall and thin hierarchy

This structure increases the company's ability to specialise its activity into divisions while also maintaining centralised management of resources. However, in recent years, there has been a trend to remove layers of management towards streamlining business. This kind of change has a direct affect on decision making because removal of task leaders requires sub-task workers to take on more decision-making responsibility themselves. Some firms have difficulty making the transition from tall and thin hierarchy to a flatter organisational structure because this change also requires a change in attitude towards employees and also sufficient training to enable the assumption of greater responsibility.

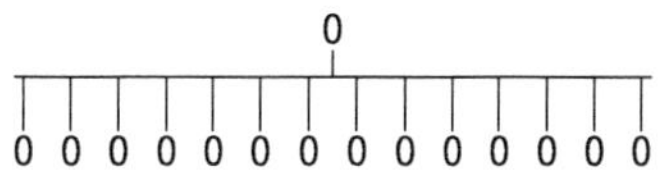

Figure 6: Flattened hierarchy model

Furthermore, the change means that a single manager becomes responsible for a larger number of staff (see Figure 6). Although cost efficient, this kind of structure has special problems in terms of communication and maintaining regular contact with staff. Particularly where managers lack supervisory experience for large teams, they will have serious difficulties when attempting to coordinate and manage enlarged departments in flatter organisations.

Using a matrix

A hierarchy is very much enhanced when it is complemented with the use of a matrix approach (see Figures 7 and 8). Applying a matrix to organise resources and information is certainly as old as hierarchy. In fact, a matrix is the underlying structure of all committees. However, its popularity and formal implementation in the twentieth century is linked to the development of the US aerospace industry during the 1960's with defense contractors seeking to qualify for US government contracts. The bidding process required them to produce proposals so that work was organised into project teams, and also to submit charts with committed personnel shown for each project along with information about their functional role in the company.

Because these companies were generally structured along functional lines such as engineering, finance, personnel, et al. the most efficient way to present the required data was to produce it as a matrix. The horizontal axis would show the functions to be included in the project and the vertical axis would feature the projects broken down into segments. This format enabled the potential client to see immediately what kind of specialist staff would be committed to each stage of the project. An example of this use of matrix can be seen in Figure 7.

Project 1	**Engineering**	**Physics**	**Administration**	**Production**
Segment A				
Segment B				
Segment C				

Figure 7: A matrix of projects to functions

Another use of the matrix format could then show the names of the personnel to be committed along the vertical axis with their specialist functions along the horizontal axis (see Figure 8).

Project 1	**Engineering**	**Physics**	**Administration**	**Production**
Project Leader	X	X		
Member A		X		
Member B				X

Figure 8: Matrix of project members to functions

A major challenge when using a matrix to organise work projects is its tendency to dilute the authority of managers in the company's hierarchy because project leaders are given a great deal of decision making authority outside the traditional hierarchy. Unless appropriate controls are in place, time and resources can be wasted if a project leader makes decisions without considering the overall needs of the company.

Critics of the hierarchical structure suggest that the matrix is more adaptable, responsive to changing environmental requirements and also more democratic. Unfortunately it also has its drawbacks. Jay Galbraith in his book, *Organisation Structure*, suggests management by matrix is the most difficult and expensive system to employ within a large organisation that has:

- high task interdependence
- changing consumer requirements
- a need to integrate large amounts of information from internal and external sources.

Greater complexity increases the need to process information and the matrix model can actually increase a company's experience of information overload.

Networks

A better approach is to blend the best features of hierarchy with those of matrix. This works because each project includes a member who has a direct link to the hierarchy and is answerable to the company's management for monitoring the project, reporting progress, addressing personnel issues, coordinating with other projects and sharing resources as needed.

Organisation and structure checklist

The following questions focus on structural issues:

1. Every organisation has a structure usually represented by an organisational chart. On occasion this chart doesn't mirror the actual roles and managerial relationships that exist in the company. Please sketch a chart that accurately describes the way your company is really organised.
2. Are the lines of authority obvious at a glance?
3. Where could there be a lack of clarity in roles and functions?
4. Does everyone know where they 'fit' in the organisation and to whom they report?
5. Does everyone know to whom they should go to offer good ideas, gain information or make complaints?
6. Which areas of the organisation are in need of assessment, reorganisation and review?

Influences on structure

There are four factors which influence the way that organisations are structured and therefore have an impact on decision making effectiveness.These are:

- the organisation's size
- the technology it uses
- its overall strategy
- the environment.

Size

Organisations are social units made up of people going about their business. Size can enhance or detract from their ability to achieve their goals. However, size not only refers to the number of employees, rather it can also refer to assets, capacity, or amount of activity and transactions.

Technology

This refers to hi-tech computer solutions as well as to old fashioned hand processing activity. When plans for change affect structure, the kind of technology that is used to complete the work needs to be identified and assessed for its specific benefits. New

structures do not necessarily mean new applications for technology, but this issue does have to be considered.

Strategy

The identification of organisational goals and the translation of vision into reality is the basis of strategy. Those businesses which are structured so that they enable the achievement of these goals and vision, have greater likelihood of success.

Environment

This issue addresses social, political, technological, economic and international factors, all of which need to be taken into account when designing a structure for running the business.

FINANCE

Targets - forecasts - gap analysis

What are ratios?

How ratios help

The larger context

The Z scores

chapter 8

The word 'budget' made its first appearance in fifteenth century written English in reference to a 'bag, pouch or wallet, usually of leather.' By the eighteenth century the word had gained the additional meaning of 'speaking one's mind', that is, opening one's budget. During that period, the Chancellor of the Exchequer when presenting the annual report to Parliament was said to 'open his budget' or in other words to divulge all of the pertinent information.

Throughout these early years, 'budget' continued to refer to a bag or pouch, as well, so that a person's budget held the amount of money or cash available for spending. When the budget was empty, that meant that funds were gone. The notion of overextending the budget or living on credit is a modern one which makes business life easier in some ways and far more challenging in others. Businesses with empty budgets do not necessarily close down. Occasionally, they are restored, reorganised and transformed. This is where leadership, decision making and the other business areas show most impact on finance. Numbers by themselves have little significance. It is the quality of the people who generate, use and interpret them that is most important.

Targets - forecasts - gap analysis

Targets

Success means different things to different people. When a company's directors have different goals for the business, they are also likely to have different financial targets and even preferences for how they want to measure financial success. For example, directors in a major conglomerate are often focused on earnings per share; the company founder and principle shareholder may like to use share price; the marketing director may refer to sales figures; and the financial director may prefer return on investment.

Regardless of these differences, reaching agreement to a financial target as well as a method for measuring success is essential. The target ensures that all parts of the business work towards a common goal and because this figure has been generally agreed, it can be more readily translated into different terms depending upon the audience.For example, institutional investors like to hear about the company's cash flow forecasts. Employees in a manufacturing firm may benefit from knowing that the directors want to achieve sales of a certain number of units and members of the board may prefer using turnover as a target. What is important is the commitment to a targeted goal, however it is expressed, so that the figures truly serve those who want to contribute to the business.

Having decided what form the target should take, the next step is to agree to a specific figure or set of figures. This targeted amount – whether of turnover, revenue, share price, return on investment, et al. – should be a monetary expression of the company's vision.

Vision is effectively turned into a reality when it is translated into a financial goal. For example, if vision includes expanding into new markets, then this can be quantified into a financial target representing the desired growth. An ambitious vision is reflected in an ambitious financial target.

Forecasts

While targets are based on a vision for the future, forecasts are produced by studying the firm's past and present financial performance. The forecast analyses information about how much income the firm has produced over a period of time. From this, a projection is made about how much income the firm has potential to earn in the future. This is a similar process to weather forecasting where analysts examine past and present information about the weather to predict its future behaviour.

The forecast is a measurement of the firm's momentum. The history of the company's growth gives a strong indication of its growth potential. If the firm continues as it is without change from either internal or external sources, then income can be forecasted as a continuation of the present figures. Another benefit offered by forecasts is the possible discovery of income generation and production trends, such as high and low earning periods over a span of time or consistently recurring lulls in business activity.

Emphasising the distinction between a target and a forecast is useful. The target is linked to the company's vision. The forecast shows the financial outcome if the company continues exactly as it is without new goals or adjustments to meet changing environmental circumstances. Ideally, the target is higher than the forecast. The difference between them reveals what kind and extent of action is necessary in order to fill the gap between them.

Gap analysis

A weak forecast and an ambitious target means that the business faces challenges in the years ahead. The company will need a plan of action with goals sufficiently ambitious to achieve the target. Moreover, these goals need to be well integrated within a strategic plan. Occasionally, a review of the gap between the target and forecast may cause directors to alter their target so that it is either a higher financial goal or a less challenging one. The five business areas (see page 27) offer a framework for effective goal setting towards closing the gap and achieving the target.

For example, increased income could be found by:

- using all facilities to their maximum and improving present efficiency
- offering additional services or new products
- developing new markets or stimulating renewed interest in existing markets
- improving management effectiveness and encouraging staff commitment
- adjusting budgets and tightening financial controls.

Figure 9 shows a company whose directors set a target of £10 million turnover within five years time.Their forecasted income is £3 million. If they are to achieve this target they need to develop a strategy which fills a gap of £7 million.This is a very ambitious target and in order to succeed it needs full support, the conviction that it can be achieved and some very good ideas to pull it off. If, after discussion and analysis, these directors decide that the goals they would need to set are not feasible, they can set a less ambitious target.Whatever target they decide, their long term goals would then be used to close the gap between the forecast and the target.

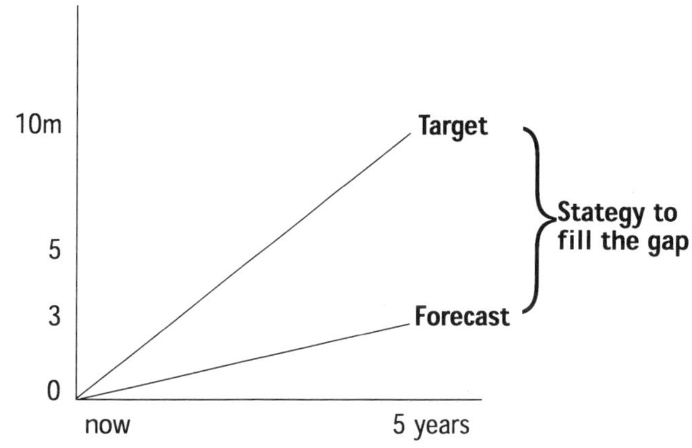

Figure 9: Identifying the gap

What are ratios?

A ratio is a comparison of any two numbers and serves as a shorthand way to show the relationship between the two. For example, 'miles per hour' or 'miles/hour' is a way to compare the number of miles that are travelled within an hour. By comparing the two numbers, a third number is produced which summarises the situation.A speed limit is one example of the use this ratio serves.The relationship between the two numbers also allows interpretations to be made about mileage and time so that 50 m.p.h. would indicate that a driver who travels for two hours will cover 100 miles, or a driver who covers 200 miles must have travelled for four hours.

When ratios are used for financial analysis, the same principle applies. Taken alone, certain financial measurements reveal little about the business. For example, knowing that a firm's current liquid income is one million doesn't really say much. That figure does become interesting, however, when it is compared to current liabilities of two million. The resulting ration of 1/2 means that for every £1 that comes in, £2 must be found to pay out for expenses.

This ratio is called the 'quick ratio' and is one way to measure the firm's viability. It compares all assets that can be easily converted into cash against those liabilities which fall due in the next operating cycle, usually a period of one year. It has been said that businesses experiencing difficulty usually have a quick ratio of less than 1 to 1, i.e. the figure for the available liquid assets is a lower number than that for the liabilities.

$$\frac{\text{cash + accounts receivable + cash equivalents}}{\text{operating cycle liabilities}} = \text{quick ratio}$$

The quick ratio is a variation of the current ratio which takes into account all of the firm's current assets and compares them to all of its current liabilities. Therefore this ratio would include non-liquid assets like prepaid rent, inventory, long-term loans and investments and compare this figure against all liabilities including mortgagees, debt, annual licenses and other long-term expenses.

$$\frac{\text{current assets}}{\text{current liabilities}} = \text{current ratio}$$

How ratios help

Ratios offer a way to analyse a company's performance. To build on the business health analogy, ratios allow analysts to check the company's 'temperature', 'weight', 'monitor its heartbeat' and in general see that all of the key indicators are in balance. Ratios are a useful spot check for managers to monitor what is going on within their business, to track its financial stability and to discover its strengths and weaknesses. Also ratios can be used to check on suppliers, competitors and others in an effective but non-invasive way. As featured in the previous section, the current and quick ratios are helpful when analysing the firm's liquidity. Other ratios are equally beneficial. Here's a list of widely used ratios which enable directors to analyse important financial data about the firm.

$$\frac{\text{cash + accounts receivable + cash equivalents}}{\text{operating cycle liabilities}} = \text{quick ratio}$$

$$\frac{\text{current assets}}{\text{current liabilities}} = \text{current ratio}$$

$$\frac{\text{accounts receivables}}{\text{sales/365}} = \text{average days collection}$$

$$\frac{\text{cost of goods sold}}{\text{average inventory}} = \text{inventory turnover}$$

$$\frac{\text{net revenues}}{\text{total assets}} = \text{assets turnover ratio}$$

$$\frac{\text{total liabilities}}{\text{total assets}} = \text{debt-to-assets ratio}$$

$$\frac{\text{gross profit}}{\text{net revenues}} = \text{gross profit margin}$$

$$\frac{\text{net income}}{\text{net revenues}} = \text{net profit margin}$$

$$\frac{\text{net income}}{\text{owners' equity}} = \text{return on investment}$$

The larger context

Ratios are indicators of financial health not a final statement. They are best examined within the larger context of the business itself and also of industry-wide activity. For example, a property development company may show high liquidity in terms of the quick ratio. However, in an industry where ownership of non-liquid tracts of land or similar investments is essential, a closer look at the company's potential would be in order if this were the case.

Three issues have particular impact on an interpretation of the ratios and act as benchmarks (see page 34) for analysing a company's performance. These are: the company's own history, a comparison with its competitors and the standards set for its industry. Company history is relevant because this takes into account the stage of the company's development. A rapidly growing company will show very different ratio results than those found in a mature company with stabilised or slow growth.

Comparing ratio results with competitors is useful as well because it leads to an analysis of why another firm may have better or worse results. Industry-wide standards enable analysts to place the company in a wider context and indicate which ratios are most relevant for that industry and what results are optimum. The challenge, though, is gathering enough accurate information to produce figures about the competition.

The Z scores

A Z-score is a formula made up of several ratios. This formula assigns a weight of importance to the ratios it includes and arrives at a single number as an outcome. This number can be used as an indicator and measure of the risk that a firm will fail financially. Two systems are prominent: E.I. Altman's and R. Toffler's. The *Bibliography* includes further reading for both of these models.

The concept of Z-scoring developed from an awareness that examining ratios in isolation gives a limited picture. In order to develop a scoring system, researchers drew upon published data from both bankrupt and healthy companies. They then applied ratios to analyse the data drawn from firms from both groups. This led to their identifying which ratios were better predictors of bankruptcy. Each ratio included in the Z-scoring formula was assigned a weight according to its relative importance based on the research. The final score gives a pass or fail mark to the company based on the Z-score criteria. For example, using the Altman's system, a Z-score above 3 is a sign of health while a score of 1.8 is dangerous. Alternatively, a pass mark using the Toffler model shows a passing Z-score would be 0. Z-scoring requires some number crunching skills, but offers a valuable predictor of financial well being.

MARKETING

Company image

Customer service

The ecology of cooperation

Unique Selling Proposition: USP

Image and USP

chapter 9

During a manufacturing firm's monthly director's meeting, the managing director highlights three points from the quarterly financial report. He says that:

1. expenditure is 15% higher than budget
2. overall sales are 20% lower
3. receipts collection is at an average of 60 days.

Everyone agrees that they must take immediate action because this situation, if ignored, could lead to serious problems. They decide that:

- all directors should make immediate cuts in their next quarter's expenses to remedy their present overspend
- the marketing director should push the sales team harder to increase orders
- the finance department should improve on collections

The directors' determination and enthusiasm for this plan creates a positive and reassuring atmosphere. Only the director of logistics who has Customer Service within his brief suggests that they haven't really addressed what may actually be *causing* the downturn in sales. This comment unsettles his colleagues. Silence falls, until the managing director responds that the sales team will just have to do a better job next quarter, 'Get those sales up', he tells the marketing director.

This scenario highlights a common blind spot about marketing. A robust marketing strategy, an excellent sales force and good products aren't necessarily enough to generate sales. Weaknesses in distribution, lack of stock, poor customer service among many other factors, all have an influence. Furthermore the company's image plays a vital part in marketing success so that when this becomes tarnished even the most determined sales force will find it difficult to generate business.

Company image

Image is an intangible asset and an important one. Every business projects an image whether company members are conscious of this or not, and this image is received by a wide variety of audiences simultaneously, including its present customers, its competition, its business allies, its own staff, government agencies, banks, local businesses, neighbours and a myriad of others. This general audience is a source of referrals, network contacts, advice, information, new business and support. From this, the company can attract and stimulate further interest from an even wider range of sources. The company can also demarket itself to all of these surrounding observers as well. Having an awareness of **how** ***the company is seen*** is very important.

Aubrey Wilson, the international marketing authority, proposes that there are four different images all of which must be managed. These are:

- **the current image:** how the firm is actually perceived
- **the mirror image:** how the firm imagines it is perceived
- **the wish image:** how the firm would like to be perceived
- **the optimum image:** how the three images can be aligned to serve the business

The current image

Information about the public's perception of the firm is essential. Anecdotal evidence or a *best guess* approach can be reassuring to directors, but is not very helpful for improving image. Inaccurate information tends to reinforce previous behaviour rather than stimulate change. The company's best source of information about its current image is from its own customers, as well as other groups such as its staff, suppliers or former customers who no longer do business with the company. This last group can be surprisingly informative if an incentive is offered, particularly if they have been dissatisfied by the firm in the past.

Information about *current image* is best gathered anonymously so that frank opinions are invited. The following set of questions provides a sample of the kind of items to be included in an image survey. They cover general issues and can be adapted in order to serve the needs of individual businesses.

Sample current image survey

1. Are you satisfied overall with the quality of the company's products/services?
2. Would you recommend this product without any qualifications or warnings?
3. Does the price of the products/services represent value for money?
4. Do you know about the company's other products and services?
5. During the last year how frequently did you make a purchase or contact the company?
6. Does the company's sales representative listen to you? Understand your needs?
7. Would you change to another company if opportunity or a better offer were made?
8. Are you kept waiting for delivery without explanation?

9. Please comment on the company's products/services in terms of the following areas:

	Poor	Adequate	Good
record keeping - documentation	____	____	____
telephone manner	____	____	____
helpfulness	____	____	____
product information	____	____	____
follow up service	____	____	____
honesty	____	____	____
courtesy	____	____	____

10. Do the company's products/services offer features which alternative suppliers lack? Please comment.

The mirror image

This refers to the way in which members of the company *imagine* how the firm is perceived. Generally this is a more flattering image than the one revealed in *current image* customer surveys. It can help improve awareness among directors if they complete the same survey which is given to customers. Their comments provide an example of a *mirror image* which can be compared to their customers' feedback. Any differences between the *current* and *mirror images* need immediate evaluation and action.

The wish image

The *wish image* refers to the way in which the company would like to be perceived. This is often linked to the highest aspirations for the company and is an ideal which encourages the pursuit of the firm's goals. A shared vision and strategy for the future contribute to the *wish image* and leads to its fulfilment.

The optimum image

This refers to alignment of all of the other images so that the firm gives a coherent and consistent message to the public. It is based on conscious choices the company has made about how it wants to serve its customers. When an *optimum image* is developed, customers are most likely to have a positive experience of the firm.

Customer service

Much is written about the importance of Customer Service. Like quality initiatives, the arguments in favour of running a 'customer centred' business are convincing to many business people until the potential costs, in terms of the time and money for evaluation, training and improvement of facilities are considered. Business leaders become more enthusiastic if they can see how their investment directly increases income.

Arthur D. Little, the international consultancy (see Appendix), has researched customer service and suggests that its benefits can be measured. The consultancy proposes that the first step is to identify what products and services customers want to buy, and then, second, what elements of service are most important to them. When specific customer needs and requests are met then the resulting increase in business is a measurable benefit. An adaptation of the Arthur D. Little approach includes the following activities:

- identify those services of vital importance to the customer through surveys and interviews
- identify the severity of customer response when this service is not offered or is poorly executed
- determine how well this service is currently offered by the firm
- identify services which customers desire but do not seek from this firm: this includes substitute products or cheaper generic versions of products
- develop a service package that includes service elements proven to influence customers

The challenge is to discover the gaps between the products and services the customer wants and those which are currently being offered by the firm. When Customer Service effort is directed towards filling this gap, then the business can benefit from improved customer satisfaction and increased sales. This takes a strategic approach to serving the customer.

The previous section offered sample questions towards discovering how customers perceived the firm. A survey can also be conducted to discover specific ways in which the company can improve its Customer Service. Its questions should focus on discovering customer *ideals of service* rather than their reactions to the company's current quality of service. Its purpose would be to identify the service and quality issues most important to the customer. However, a few information gathering items could also be included.

Directors can use the data to decide whether it's appropriate or even possible for the business to develop a package which includes these desirable elements and also to discover

to what degree the company's current services are already valued. A sample of the kind of items that could be included in this kind of survey follows:

Sample customer service survey

1. It is important that the products I buy are guaranteed.

   1 — 10

   low importance — high importance

2. It is important that I can get replacement parts easily.

   1 — 10

   low importance — high importance

3. It is important that there is a help line to ask technical questions.

   1 — 10

   low importance — high importance

4. It is important that I am able to place an order on the phone, the Internet, et al.

   1 — 10

   low importance — high importance

These are just a few of the possible items about service needs which could be included. This kind of survey is an opportunity for managers to discover what their customers want and need, their general preferences, and what they would want to get in terms of service and quality. Directors with a flexible attitude are likely to gain the most from this kind of survey. Preconceived ideas and a narrow view about what customers want can limit the ability to discover the next new trend or develop a sharper edge over the competition.

The ecology of cooperation

James Moore, a Massachusetts-based consultant proposes that technological advances have contributed to a radical change in the nature of competition. He describes a strategy of developing markets and gaining new business through using networks of contacts. These are clusters of businesses which work together to provide mutual support in a systematic

way. This approach challenges the idea that marketing means a head to head contest with the competition to win a client's business or acquire a project contract. Networking is a more subtle form of promotion so that new business results through contact with a wide variety of industries and related businesses.

These contacts are nourished through regular exchange of ideas, knowledge and pursuit of innovative ways to do business. This approach to business development is as old as the act of bartering goods. It is of particular value in today's market place because computer technology has increased the ability of firms to make links in order to share data and so speed marketing decisions. The following questions are designed to evaluate contacts towards discovering if they could be potential allies for network marketing. Positive answers would indicate that a targeted company deserves further investigation.

- Does the company offer products/services which complement ours?
- What markets does this company have in addition to our own?
- Is this company already positioned in a market we want to enter?
- Are we already positioned in a market useful to the the other company?
- Do any of the directors share common ground with directors from the other company in terms of social background, work experience, education, etc.?

Unique Selling Proposition: USP

To gain the maximum benefit from participating in a network, a firm needs a strong identity. Giving and receiving support through links with other companies means each business in the network has to be equally robust. The *unique selling proposition* (USP) is also referred to as *distinctive competence*, *market edge* or *market advantage*, and is a statement that identifies an essential company strength which both satisfies a customer demand and, at the same time, provides an advantage over the competition. Although every company has many strengths, the USP is a specific strength which sets the business apart and makes customers return to it rather than go to the competition. It is a major contributor to the company's image.

The identification of USP begins by making an inventory of all the company's strengths. This list is then assessed in terms of how customers respond to the company using data from *current image* surveys as far as is possible. At first, the USP may remain unclear even after long discussion. However, once the it is identified then the directors have a powerful selling tool and a means to communicate to those both inside and outside the business about what makes the company special. Its discovery is helped if directors identify with their customers towards thoroughly understanding what makes them choose the company's products over all of the others.

Analysing the competition

Defining a company's USP means getting to know and understand the competition. The following questions focus on analysing the competition towards recognising any crucial differences.

1. How many competing firms are there in the company's area:
    - local?
    - regional?
    - national
2. Of these how many are:
    - larger?
    - the same size?
    - smaller?
3. What are the specific characteristics of each of these firms?
4. Which firms are significant competitors?
5. Which firms offer a similar product or service?
6. What kind of customers are drawn to these firms? How would you distinguish them from the company's customers?
7. List the distinguishing traits of the competition. Include those features that are the same as the company's.
8. How is each competitor different from the company, in either a positive or negative way?
9. What additional information is needed in order to understand the competition better?

USP summary

In summary this is the sequence to follow to identify USP:

- gather data about customer ideals and reactions to the company
- list the company's strengths
- decide which of these directly meets a demand for service
- gather data about the competition's strengths and weaknesses
- identify how this service gives an advantage over the competition.

Image and USP

Figure 11 illustrates that a positive image and clearly defined USP attracts customers from the general public. In Phase 1 the company provides excellent products and services, and this positive image is reinforced for these customers. This leads in turn to Phase 2 where these customers recommend the firm to others so that the image and USP are further reinforced.

Alternatively, Figure 12 shows the effects of a negative or an unclear image and a lack of USP upon a company's ability to attract new business. The negative outcomes from Phase 1 of this situation are aggravated further in Phase 2 if the customers who do try the company's products then have a negative experience. This leads to even fewer, if any referrals.

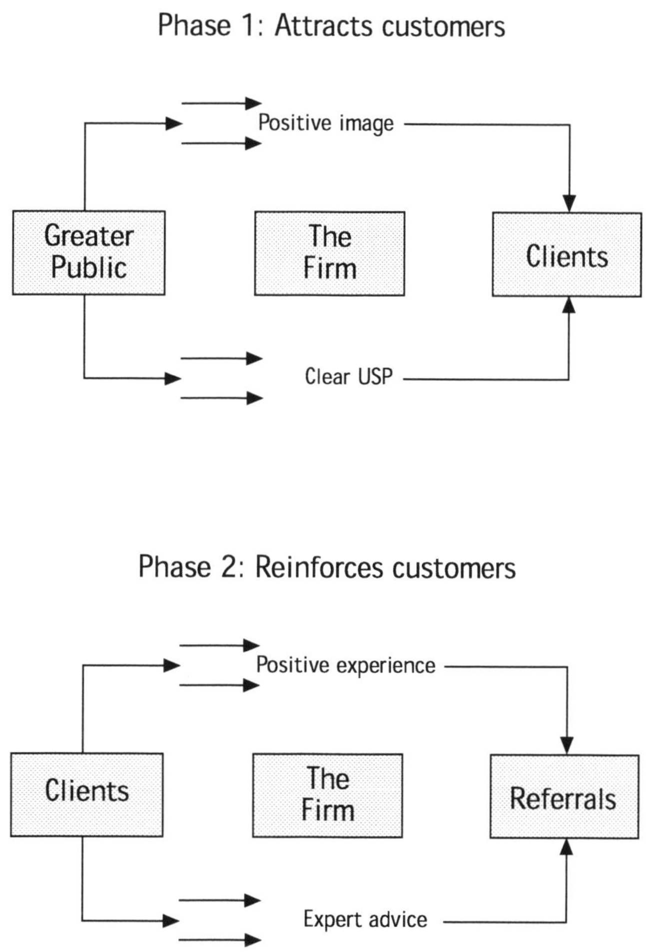

Figure 10: Positive image

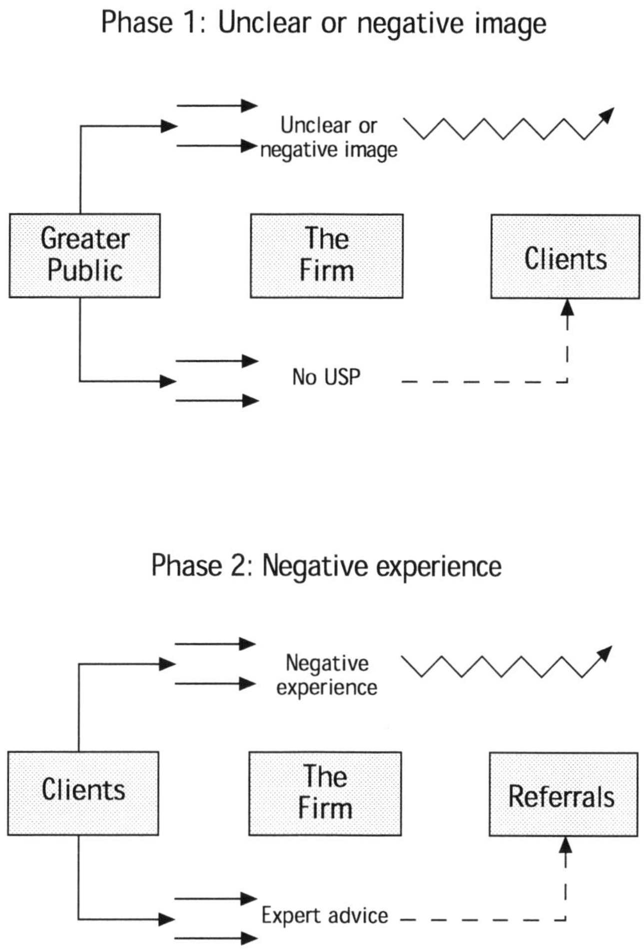

Figure 11: Negative image

COMMUNICATION

chapter 10

This chapter addresses two levels of communication needs for business. First, there are the personal skills which company members need in order to exchange information clearly and effectively. Second, there is the company's system of communication which enables the flow of information to occur. Both levels are important and are best analysed separately in order to create company-wide improvement.

Part 1: personal skills

Bypassing

Two managers are travelling together to meet an important new sales contact. One of the managers looks up from his papers and asks the other,'Did you get the fax?' His colleague answers, 'Yes, thank you for that information.' to which the first responds, 'Well, what did you think?'The second answers,'Very helpful, thank you.', and then they both return to their reading.

At a critical point during the meeting which follows, the potential buyer asks a question. The two managers answer simultaneously with one saying 'yes' and the other saying 'no'. After the meeting the first manager angrily asks his colleague why he gave the client that answer when the fax he said he'd read contained all of the necessary background information.They then discover that they had been referring to different faxes.The moral of the story is this: it's tempting to assume that agreements are based on complete understanding, but this is as rare as it is unlikely. Assumptions about what other people mean are only guesses in disguise.

This kind of miscommunication is called *bypassing* and is caused by people giving different meanings to the same words. It occurs on a daily basis and is often discovered only after misunderstandings emerge. Bypassing occurs because:

- meaning is inside people rather than within the words themselves
- stress impacts communication
- communication is difficult.

Meaning is inside people

Background, education, personality all contribute to the ways in which people interpret what they hear. Self-awareness is the key to effective communication because it leads

managers to notice other people's reactions to what they are saying. Frequently, there are clear signals that miscommunication is occurring, such as surprising answers to obvious questions, puzzled facial expressions, hesitancy and a careful choice of words. Any of these signs can indicate bypassing; unfortunately, they are often ignored.

Stress impacts communication

Stressful situations and feelings can lead managers to use a style of communication that is more extreme than the one they normally use. When under stress they may give information in a stronger and more assertive way, or alternatively, they may become more hesitant, vague and withdrawn. This is seen in everyday life as the nervous reaction before meeting the boss or making a presentation to the board. Although this behaviour is generally considered to be normal, its impact on clear communication is negative and often, because of it, listeners are misled about the significance of what they are hearing.

Communication is difficult

Because managers have been communicating with relative success throughout their lives, this very complex skill is generally taken for granted. There is nothing more difficult than getting meaning across to another person. Ironically, it is the frequency of miscommunication, its seeming harmlessness and the fluid ways people fix their mistakes that makes it easy to take communication skill – or its lack – for granted. Tone of voice, inflexion and knowledge of the speaker all contribute to an accurate interpretation of what is being said. When speaking and listening, it helps to remember that any single message can be interpreted as:

- a direction
- a request
- a suggestion
- a piece of information
- a question.

Social skills

Managers, especially at senior levels need skill to inspire confidence, encourage their staff and peers and also ensure that their own personalities are not getting in the way of their being understood. Owen Hargie is a communication expert and academic at the University of Ulster. He suggests that there are recognisable features which contribute to socially skilled behaviour and, therefore to communication effectiveness.

An adaptation of his work highlights five social skills:

1. goal directed
2. coherent
3. appropriate to the situation
4. learned
5. controlled

Managers with excellent communication skills demonstrate all of these features, but this achievement takes years of practice, trial and error and determination. Those who seriously want to improve their communication success rate, can use the five social skills as guides. The skills also provide a means for evaluating a manager's communication performance and for this a series of *Diagnostic Questions* follow this section.

Goal directed

This skill enables managers to identify and concentrate on achieving a specific outcome when they initiate contact with others. For example, there is the manager who meets with a customer to gain information and therefore directs all of the discussion towards that end. Although they may also discuss other issues, the manager does not lose sight of the initial goal and considers the interaction a success only when this is achieved.

Coherent

With this skill managers behave so that they make a single harmonious impression. For example, it is seen in the discussion leader who uses gestures, words, facial expression and eye contact harmoniously when leading a meeting. This fluid performance gives an overall impression of concentration and skill.

Appropriate to the situation

This skill presents itself when managers recognise the need to match their behaviour to the needs of each situation. For example, the manager who reserves expressing frustration towards a staff member when in the presence of others or who uses laughter to encourage a stressed and tired team to finish a project on time.

Learned

Here managers take on and integrate new communication behaviour through observation and study. For example, the manager who copies a much admired boss or attends a seminar towards consciously changing communication style and behaviour, then practices until new skills are attained.

Controlled

Control is a skill which allows managers to time their behaviour and choose how to express themselves. For example, the supervisor who listens to a trainee staff member carefully, only intervening to ask a question or give necessary advice towards the trainee's gaining confidence and learning how to complete the task independently.

Making an impact: diagnostic questions

The following questions can be used to evaluate communication performance after important meetings and sessions. Self-evaluation and review enables managers to build on mistakes and strengthen their social skills for the next time.

1. What was the purpose for this discussion? Did I achieve this? Did I consciously change the purpose of the discussion?
2. How did I know that I had achieved my purpose? What feedback from my listener gave me this information?
3. Was there anything about my behaviour or appearance which may have created an uncoordinated impression? For example:
   - style of dress
   - language or phrasing
   - demonstration of expertise
   - eye contact
   - impact of age, gender or race
   - personal mannerisms.
4. What signs did I use to identify the situation's changing needs? How well did I adapt to the situation?
5. Did the listener indicate that I provided the information which was needed? What signals were used? How did I interpret them?

6. Did I pace my behaviour so that the other person could understand what I was saying? Did I present my ideas so the other person was interested from first to last?
7. What, if any, past experiences were similar to this situation? Did I learn anything from the past?

Rich communication

Communication is an exchange of messages requiring at least one sender and one receiver and can be either verbal or non-verbal. When communication occurs between socially skilled individuals, there is an increased likelihood that clear, accurate and meaningful messages are exchanged and that misunderstandings are likely to be corrected with least upset when they do occur. Alternatively, when communication is based upon only an assumption of understanding and is superficially managed, then virtually anything can happen.

Consider making a routine request to a staff member for a file. Seemingly the only requirement for successful communication is the provision of a name or number for the file. However, this simple request may be executed using a variety of methods, including electronic transmission, telephone, face to face contact or written memo, and mistakes can easily occur at even this initial stage. In addition, misunderstandings potentially arise about urgency, format needs (diskette, computer screen, paper copies) and place of delivery, among many other considerations. As messages become more complicated, the potential for serious mishap increases in relation to this complexity.

Therefore any exchange of vital information requires careful consideration with communication experts suggesting that managers use *rich* methods of communication. This term refers to the amount of meaning that can be conveyed through the message. Some methods offer limited opportunity to express meaning while others enable a manager to get subtle and intricate messages across successfully. There are three basic communication methods each of which offer different *richness* opportunities. These are:

- **written:** in English there are 29 symbols (26 letters and 3 major punctuation marks)
- **vocal:** in English there are 32 phonemes (sounds) with variations provided by pitch, tone, accent and pause
- **visual and vocal:** this includes all of the vocal variations as well gestures, eye contact, and bodily positioning.

Because written communication provides least opportunity for expressing subtlety, it is less helpful when nuance must be conveyed or sensitivity is required. For example, it can seem efficient to use e-mail to send a letter of rejection or transmit other unhappy news, but this is potentially wounding to the recipient. Method does matter, and managers reveal a great deal about their communication skills through the methods they choose to communicate difficult information. However, written communication is necessary when:

- there is a great deal of information
- accuracy and detail are crucial
- many people will receive the same message
- a record or history of the contact is needed
- the message goes beyond the initial recipient
- confirmation of receipt or follow-up is necessary.

Voice to voice contact on the telephone offers a compromise between face to face and written communication. However, there can be no substitute for face to face contact when there are emotions involved. Physical presence communicates subtle information about the speaker's meaning and when richness is required, this should be the method of choice.

Right and left brain thinking

Edward de Bono, the communication expert, has written a great deal about left and right brain thinking. He suggests that there are two kinds of thinkers both of whom use very different styles of communicating.Communication effectiveness can increase when managers understand these differences and also know how best to work with those who think differently. Left brain people are called linear (or vertical) thinkers. Right brain people are called lateral thinkers

Linear

This kind of thinking is analytical and focuses on how the separate parts of an idea fit together. Solutions to problems are developed by discovering what doesn't fit or what is missing.These thinkers often get new ideas by taking old ones apart and reorganising them. They work logically and sequentially.

Lateral

This kind of thinking is intuitive and allows ideas to emerge after studying a number of separate possibilities. Solutions to problems are developed by discovering new ways to

connect these separate possibilities. This means discarding some and redefining others in the quest for a new way of thinking. Lateral thinkers focus on the relationships of the parts to the whole.

A comparison

Linear thinkers tend to consider laterals to be superficial, imprecise and careless. Lateral thinkers can believe linears to be slow reacting, over cautious and weighed down with detail. When working together the two kinds of thinkers emphasis different features of a problem and have very different ways of prioritising what needs to be done. For example, linear thinkers would work their way through a Briefing such as this from the first chapter to the last. A lateral thinker would dip into those sections which seem most relevant and progress through the Briefing by linking one topic to the another. Both approaches have much to offer and skilful communicators can choose to develop both lateral and linear thinking abilities.

Listening

Listening has three essentials:

1. bias awareness
2. visual signals
3. vocal signals.

Bias awareness

There are people who insist they have no biases. This is impossible because of the nature of human perception. All information is filtered through the senses and interpreted by individual personalities. Even those with similar backgrounds, family history, taste and talents can interpret what they see and hear very differently. This is bias, and managers particularly need to recognise and understand their own.

Visual signals

This is also called body language and great care must be used when interpreting it. There are many books and seminars available which are sincere attempts to make sense of this form of human exchange, but in a multicultural society a universal code cannot be fully available. The only course for skilled professionals is **to ask** what a colleague means by an ambiguous gesture. Guesswork can cause serious misunderstandings and unnecessary error.

Vocal signals

This is the most obvious form of listening and should include hearing what is not said as well as what is. Also listeners benefit by asking themselves whether the tone of voice matches the content of what is being said. It takes skill to identify the unexpressed emotional state behind the words. Subtle messages are often discovered in tone, pitch, breathing and delivery style, an awareness of which aids understanding.

Speaking

Speaking has three essentials:

1. headlining
2. pacing
3. summarising.

Headlining

This is similar to giving a news headline at the outset of speaking. With practice it becomes a natural way to emphasise the most important points of what is about to be said. Headlines are an antidote to long rambling stories which never seem to get anywhere and is an essential skill for managers seeking to influence others.

Pacing

This refers to the speed and sense of rhythm used to deliver a message. It also means that a speaker knows when to stop talking and invite the other person to speak. A necessary learning point for those senior managers who routinely cut others off having assumed that their greater authority justifies this kind of behaviour. During well paced communication, speakers tend to pause after completing a headline and then wait to hear comments from their listeners before they continue speaking themselves.

Summarising

This technique is a skilful integration of all the headlines included during the communication session. It means paraphrasing the content briefly so that it invites further comment or questions from the listeners. It fits most naturally into a discussion just as a topic is being changed or as a conversation slows down. This technique is particularly useful when important information is being presented and there is a particular need for clarity.

Part 2: organisational issues

The first part of this chapter addressed the skills and issues necessary for effective communication, person to person. This section features the need for information to move, be transferred or flow in a systematic way throughout the company.

Information flow

There are five ways that this information flow typically occurs. They are: the circle, the all-channel, the 'Y', the wheel and the chain.

Circle and all-channel

Circle and all-channel

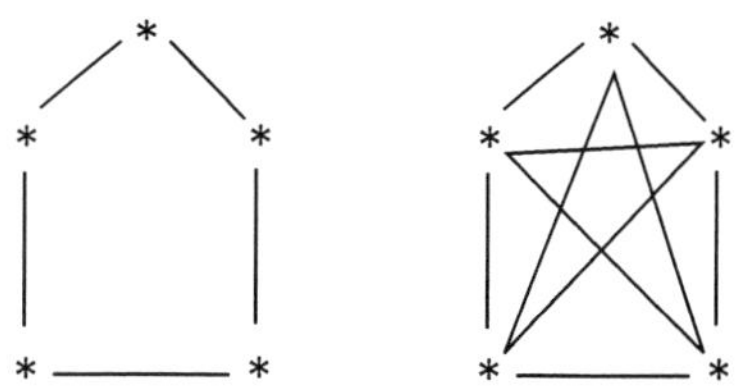

The circle The all-channel

Both of these diagrams show systems which give company members an opportunity to interact and exchange information with each other as required. They also tend to encourage members of the system to share responsibility and take initiative. However, the *circle* and *all-channel* can be time-consuming and require more resources for completion of complex tasks. The end result, though, is often increased accuracy.

'Y' and Chain

'Y' and chain

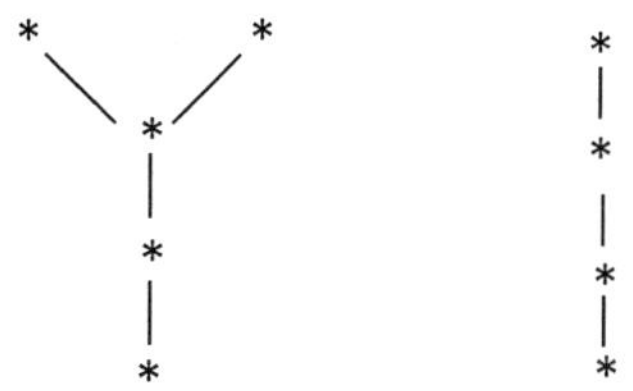

The 'Y' The chain

The *'Y'* and the *chain* offer more centralised control over information flow and are associated with traditional business relationships between managers and subordinates. In general, these models are beneficial for simple tasks where speed of information transfer is important. They also offer greater accuracy when messages are simple and straightforward.

Wheel

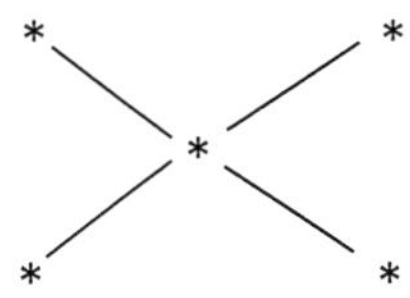

The wheel

The *wheel* shows the most centralised communication system with the person at the centre making contact with all of the the members on the spokes of the wheel, and those on the spokes contacting the others only through the central person.

Summary

There are research findings that the *'Y'*, the *chain* and the *wheel* can hinder organisational innovation and change. The sequential transfer of information slows the exchange of both ideas and vital information so that discussion, debate and data exchange can become a costly and error ridden process. The *all-channel* and *circle* models are particularly helpful when communicating information about change and when ideas need to be exchanged freely. A well balanced communication system matches the right model to the needs of each situation.

Roles

Each member of an organisation has a role within the communication system. These roles have a strong influence on the way that information flows though the organisation.

Gatekeepers

Gatekeepers pass information on to others and control its flow as part of their job. Although this is a very important function, relatively low status employees often serve in this role, such as telephone operators and receptionists. They are often found at the hub of a *wheel* communication model.

Liaisons

This refers to staff who provide links between groups within the organisation. These roles imply gatekeeping, but it is their primary responsibility to increase information flow and coordinate contact between differing groups.

Opinion leaders

These are influential people regardless of their job title or status in the business. Frequently they have informal influence and can be *proactive*, offering their opinions without being asked or *reactive*, waiting until they are asked before they give their views.

Isolates

These are individuals with few contacts in the organisation and little influence.

Participants

This refers to individuals with many contacts who actively take part in the communication stream.

Communication channels checklist

This checklist focuses on analysing the way that communication occurs within an organisation.

1. How many levels to the organisation? How many departments?
2. Consider how information would flow through the organisation in an ideal situation.
3. Consider how information flows in reality.
4. Consider where any blocks to this flow could occur.
5. Consider how these blocks could impact implementation of new ideas.
6. Draw a diagram of how information about a major change would be communicated throughout the business.

Directors can answer these questions first as individuals and then later discuss their results together with colleagues. The purpose is discovery of potential weaknesses towards bringing the communication system into maximum effectiveness.

INFORMATION TECHNOLOGY: IT

The intranet

Data storage and management

Traditional versus Web enabled storage

The Internet

Developing a selling site

Security

chapter 11

Information is a source of power. It leads to the discovery of new markets, products and ways of managing people and resources. It also provides the means to analyse the competition and maintain a presence in the market-place. However, information can also heighten rivalry within organisations because the choice to give, receive and withhold information provides a source of considerable power to those who know how to use it. This was true before the electronic revolution and is now even more relevant with new technology developments.

Ironically, an example of information hoarding is often found in IT departments themselves. The popularity of the Internet for e-mail and Web access, as well as the arrival to the workplace of the first computer literate generations, have increased users' sophistication. Formerly IT managers had guru-like status, now some of them struggle to meet new levels of user demand. This erosion of power causes some IT managers to refuse innovative database solutions, Internet links and even e-mail development.

Those responsible for making budgetary decisions for technology have to address this kind of leadership issue as well as identify the company's technology needs. Successful IT developments can be a major factor towards achieving company vision. There are four IT issues of particular relevance in todays' market place:

- Intranet development
- Document storage and management
- Internet links
- Security.

Intranet development refers to both equipment purchase and software which is designed specifically for a company's use. Efficient management and storage of documents is important because it makes information readily accessible and can give the business a significant advantage in terms of time, labour and cost savings. The company's link to the Internet is another vital issue because it enables fast, inexpensive global communication and marketing opportunities. Finally, security systems which protect the company's privacy include human issues of training, commitment to the firm and personal awareness as well as technology development.

The intranet

A recent survey by Smythe Dorwood Lambert (see Appendix) suggests that 60% of the UK's top businesses have either developed an intranet or are in the process of doing so. It is considered by decision makers to be an important trend in communication technology and

is also believed to be a means to cut costs and improve efficiency.The survey includes data from 269 responses to a questionnaire sent to 1,760 members of *The Times* 'Top 500 Companies'. Other findings show that e-mail has now overtaken the fax as a cost-saving communication method, and that open sharing of business information through an intranet is considered desirable by only 10% of the respondents.

So what is an intranet and what can it do? In its widest sense an intranet is a system of interlinked computers whose activities are coordinated by a more powerful computer called a server. Many company's already have the basis of an intranet through mid-1990's investments in Local Area Networks (LAN). However, new technology offers vastly improved speed, user to user communication features and data access lacking in the early LAN's.

Intranet technology owes much to the World Wide Web (the Web or WWW), now a household word.The Web (see Appendix) was originally developed by an English physicist, Tim Berners-Lee, who one day in 1989 turned to his colleagues and said, wouldn't it be nice to be able to access any document in the world just by pressing a button. It was then that he decided to write the code that eventually enabled the present day Web to emerge. It is the Web's capacity to open the doors to a world-wide source of information in a user friendly way that has captured people's imaginations in a manner that the Internet alone could not achieve.

Intranets are based on the same principles which underlie the Web: that any document stored in a network and assigned a locator address can be accessed through any other document as long as they are all linked and share an address system. A well designed Intranet gives users access to records, memo's and departmental information stored for general use by other users in that network.This means that sales, financial, personnel and production information can be viewed on a screen and printed by any member of staff whether in-house or on the road.

It also means that departments can offer summaries and highlights of their work so that they can inform their colleagues about current trends and issues. Potentially, intranets transform the ways that employees communicate internally and can simplify serving customers and managing products and sales.

Intranets can and should be designed to meet the special needs of each company.There are now software solutions that promise an ability to have an intranet 'up and running in the same day'. In fact, intranet development requires considerable investment of time and money if it is to offer real benefit to the business.This is because an internal network of links across all functions, projects and departments means rethinking the way that

documents are stored, filed and used and also requires anticipating future business growth as well as training, equipment and software needs.

Data storage and management

Any business with more than one computer needs to plan data storage so that information can be accessed easily. As computer and user numbers increase an effective strategy becomes even more essential. An intranet can be designed so that it addresses data management needs. However, there are issues specific to storage and data access that need attention first so that the system can be fully integrated into an intranet. Key issues to be addressed include:

1. What kind of data does the firm generate?
2. How is data organised now: by function, department, project, individuals?
3. Is this the best way to organise your business data in terms of:
   - who needs access?
   - what purpose does the data serve (archives, reference, research)?
   - what new purposes could data storage serve?
4. What are the security issues: which staff should access what data?
5. In what ways can effective data management help company members get the information they need for:
   - sales and marketing?
   - staff development and administrative planning?
   - budget decisions?

Traditional versus Web enabled storage

Traditional data management offers a powerful and straightforward means of accessing data using long-developed database techniques. An alternative is now available which is based on the technology developed for the Web so that documents are stored within a network of other documents. This network approach allows users to search for information *related to* a document as well as for a document itself. This is possible because data is initially stored in such a way that its relationship to other data is taken into account with links made across, between and throughout all of the documents as they are being stored. It is an attractive option because it enables fast access to whole topics of information rather than to isolated documents.

Although software designers are enthusiastic about this innovation and the many benefits that it offers, they also warn developers of potential problems. Web style document management is less suited to businesses with a long history of data storage and extensive archives. System designers need to take particular care to avoid creating inaccessible islands of data which can neither talk to each other nor to a newly installed Web-style system.

They recommend instead an 'interoperable' system which blends traditional and Web-enabled data management. This compromise offers both access to older data with the potential of integrating this into a system based on network technology. Companies wishing to integrate its databases into an intranet can benefit because a Web-style system which cooperates with a traditional approach can link directly into an intranet.

The Internet

The Internet, or Net, is a collection of fully independent computer networks located around the world. Together they form a network of networks each responsible for its own administration and maintenance. Internet research guru, Mark Lotter (see Appendix) suggests that there are now over 16.1 million connected computers in 176 countries making the Internet's apparent growth rate about 70% per year.

AOL a major Internet service provider in the US and UK reports that its customers are:

- 70% aged between 35 and 64
- 58% earning above £25,000
- 89% owning their own homes.

These results reveal that the Internet presents a desirable population for vendors and a source of potential sales for those with the skill to use the Internet to promote their products and services. The main criteria for successful Internet selling is a willingness to reconsider customers' behaviour in terms of what attracts them to a product or service, and also what information they want about it before they choose to buy.

This means taking a different approach from that used in conventional media. Conventional advertising campaigns depend upon catching a potential customer's eye through magazines, newspapers and television. With the Internet, customers must be drawn to visit a site in order to discover more about a product or company. This is often achieved by offering value added information services such as the automobile association which gives traffic updates or the cosmetic company which provides fashion and make-up ideas.

The Internet potentially transforms selling efforts because the technology allows a business to focus intently on an individual customer's interests without the expense which normally goes along with such personalised service. The following points highlight which features lead to successful Internet selling and which do not.

Key features of success

- identifying what information customers really want to know
- focusing on customers' convenience
- giving an exclusive service
- using technology to pioneer new services
- turning information about products into a new and valued service.

Key features of failure

- disregarding the customers' needs
- annoying customers with uninteresting information
- slow access to sites due to poor design
- misjudging the value customers give to a product
- failing to enhance the product with added and desired information.

Developing a selling site

An Internet sales promotion is usually referred to as a **home page** or a Web site. Some companies make the error of using their current business brochure as a basis for their site and others go to the opposite extreme and produce an all-singing and all-dancing effort. The best approach is somewhere in the middle. A careful look at what the company wants to achieve through an Internet connection often leads to the priority setting necessary to decide what content to include. The following questions highlight the issues which need attention when developing a home page.

1. What products should be promoted and how should they be described?
2. What company information should be highlighted?
3. Is there a special service or entertainment feature which can be offered?
4. What pictures, graphics and colours suit your company best?
5. What degree of interaction with customers is appropriate?
6. What methods can be used to gather customer comments?

Evaluating the site

When the site is complete and before launching it onto the Web, it needs a thorough evaluation. Feedback can be gathered from staff at all levels of the business as a means to anticipate its reception by *Web surfers* and viewers.

1. Is the overall tone positive and in line with the company's values and ideas?
2. Is there a clear connection between what the company has to offer and the information service being presented on the page?
3. Are any games actually fun to play?
4. Are customers likely to be interested in the included facts, graphs and charts?
5. Are the links and references to other parts of the site likely to interest customers?
6. Can they easily understand how to use these links to connect to the other parts?

Security

Computer security refers to maintenance of a stable, consistent, uninterrupted service; in fact, whatever measures are required to secure an electronic system so that it can be managed to the standard and intentions of its owners. The 1998 *Business Information Security Survey* (BISS) conducted by the National Computing Centre and sponsored by the Department of Trade and Industry (see Appendix) shows that 44% of respondents reported incidents of security breach. This is a marked increase from the 1994 survey results of 9% and the 1996 results of 16%. These breaches fall into two categories: physical and logical with theft and viruses representing the most common occurrences of misuse in each category. Other physical breach issues include power failure, Local Area Network (LAN) failure, fire and sabotage. Additional logical breaches feature user error, staff misuse, software copyright and fraud.

A security breach can come from inside the firm through the actions of current or past employees or temporary contractors; or from outside the business through hackers, competitors or random criminal attack. Although new legislation is underway to safeguard business data, legal action after a breach is made provides little consolation for a disrupted business and loss of vital data. The best course of action is to assume the worst and close every loophole. This means investing in the kind of equipment and software which carefully monitors the system so intruders set off an electronic alarm and can then be traced. The more a firm depends upon its data, the more it needs sophisticated security measures.

Experts recommend that businesses establish policies for computer use as well as work environment security. Areas for discussion include:

- access to data
- authorised use of equipment, including attachment of modems and other personal devices to company computers
- copyright: ownership of stored information
- confidentiality
- backup routines
- authorised keys and building entry code information.

The British Standards Institution offers a standard for establishing and maintaining the security of electronic systems (see Appendix). It is BS7799 (part 2), *Specifications For Security Management Systems.*

REFERENCES

appendix 1

Vision in Practice Ltd.
Carol A. O'Connor, Ph D
23 Belsize Park Gardens
London NW3 4JH

http://www.visiprac.com telephone: 0171-483-2752

Page 17

Winning
Department of Trade and Industry
Management Best Practice Directorate
4th Floor
1 Victoria Street
London SW1H 0ET telephone: 0870-150-2500 (to order copies)

Page 34

BS 7850 Part 2:
Total Quality Management: Guidelines for Quality Improvement
British Standards Institution
2 Park Street
London W1A 2BS telephone: 0171-629-9000

Page 51

Developing Businesses Through Developing Individuals
by D. Butcher, P. Harvey and S. Atkinson
Cranfield School of Management
Cranfield University
Cranfield
Bedford MK43 0AL telephone: 01234-751122

Page 69

Measuring the Payoff from Improved Customer Service
by Harvey N. Shycon
Arthur D. Little
Berkeley Square House
Berkeley Square
London W1X 6EY telephone: 0171-491-8983

Page 88

Communication Futures: Technology
Symthe Dorwood Lambert
Communication Management Consultancy
55 Drury Lane
London WC2B 5SQ

www.smythe.co.uk telephone: 0171-379-9099

Page 89

World Wide Web Consortium

http://www.w3.org

An international organisation which brings together experts from leading computer and software companies, world renowned computer laboratories and members of other Internet task force teams. It develops and promotes common standards for World Wide Web initiatives.

Page 91

Mark K. Lotter
Network Wizards
P.O. Box 343
Menlo Park, CA 94026

http://www.nw.com telephone: 650-326-2060

Network Wizards has been conducting a twice annual survey of the Internet since 1990. The company publishes reports and provides a range of services for Internet users.

Page 93

Business Information Security Survey (BISS): 1998
National Computing Centre Ltd.
Oxford House
Oxford Road
Manchester M1 7ED telephone: 0161-228-6333

Page 94

BS 7799 Part 2: Specifications for Security Management Systems
British Standards Institution
2 Park Street
London W1A 2BS telephone: 0171-629-9000

BIBLIOGRAPHY

appendix 2

Altman, E. I. and McGough, T.P., 'Evaluation of a Company as a Going Concern', *Journal of Accountancy*, Dec. 1974.

Argenti, John, *Practical Corporate Planning.* London: Unwin Hyman, 1989.

Argenti, John, *Predicting Corporate Failure.* London: Institute of Chartered Accountants in England and Wales, 1984.

Barrett, Neil, *The State of Cybernation: Cultural, Political and Economic Implications of the Internet.* London: Kogan Page, 1996.

Bazerman, Max, *Judgement in Managerial Decision Making.* New York: Wiley, 1980.

Bennis, Warren, *On Becoming a Leader*, Reading, MA: Addision-Wesley, 1989.

Burns, James MacGregor, *Leadership.* New York: Harper & Row, 1978.

Butcher, D., Harvey, P., and Atkinson, S., 'Developing Businesses Through Developing Individuals', Research Report. Cranfield, UK: University of Cranfield, 1997.

Camp, Robert, *Business Process Benchmarking: Finding and Implementing Best Practices.* Wilwaukee, WI: American Society for Quality Control Press, 1995.

de Bono, Edward, *Lateral Thinking: A Textbook of Creativity.* London: Penguin, 1977.

Department of Trade and Industry, *Winning* (revised), London: DTI, 1997.

Galbraith, Jay R., *Organization Structure.* Reading, MA: Addision-Wesley, 1977.

Hargie, Owen (ed.), *A Handbook of Communication Skills*, London: Routledge, 1986.

Hersey, Paul and Blanchard, Kenneth H., *Management of Organizational Behaviour: Utilising Human Resources.* Englewood Cliffs, NJ: Prentice-Hall, 1977.

Lewin, Kurt, Lippitt, Ronald and White, Ralph, 'Patterns of Aggressive Behaviour in Experimentally Created Social Climates', *Journal of Social Psychology*, 10, 271-99, 1939.

Minzberg, Henry, *The Rise and Fall of Strategic Planning.* Free Press, 1994.

Moore, James F., 'Predators and Prey: a New Ecology of Competition', *Harvard Business Review*, 71, 3, 75-86, 1993.

National Computing Centre, 'Business Information Security Survey: 1998,' Research Report. Manchester, UK: NCC, 1998.

O'Connor, Carol A., *The Handbook for Organizational Change*. McGraw-Hill, 1993.

O'Connor, Carol A., *Successful Selling on the Internet*. London: Hodder Headline, 1996.

Schein, Edgar H., 'Culture Matters', *Demos*, 8, pp. 38-39, 1996.

Shycon, Harvey K., 'Measuring the Payoff from Improved Customer Relations', *Prism*, 1, 71-81, 1991, Arthur D. Little, Cambridge, MA.

Smythe Dorwood Lambert, 'Communication Futures: Technology', Research Report. *Perspectives*, 1997.

Sullivan, Jerry, Kameda, Naoki, and Nobu, Tatsuo, 'Bypassing in Managerial Communication', *Business Horizons*, 34 (1), 71-80, 1991.

Taffler, R. and Tishaw, H., 'Going, Going, Gone – Four Factors which Predict', *Accountancy*, March 1977.

Westwick, C.A., *How to Use Management Ratios*. London: Gower, 1987.

Wilson, Aubrey, *Emancipating the Professions*. London: John Wiley & Sons, 1994.

Wilson, Aubrey, *The Marketing of Professional Services*. London: McGraw-Hill, 1972.